The Friendship Factor

**HOW TO GET CLOSER
TO THE PEOPLE
YOU CARE FOR**

ALAN LOY MCGINNIS

Augsburg Books
MINNEAPOLIS

Also by Dr. Alan Loy McGinnis

The Romance Factor (New York: HarperColins, 1982, distributed by Dickinson Publishing Group, Seattle and Glendale)

Bringing Out the Best in People (Minneapolis: Augsburg, 1985)

Confidence (Minneapolis: Augsburg, 1987)

The Power of Optimism (New York: HarperColins, 1990, distributed by Dickinson Publishing Group, Seattle and Glendale)

The Balanced Life (Minneapolis: Augsburg, 1995, distributed by Dickinson Publishing Group, Seattle and Glendale)

Editions of *The Friendship Factor* have been published by Claretian (Philippines), Glad Sounds (Malaysia and Singapore), Hodder and Stoughton (U.K.), Lutheran Publishing House (Australia and New Zealand), St. Paul's (India, Pakistan, Sri Lanka).

The book has also been translated into Afrikaans, Chinese, Dutch, Finnish, French, German, Hindi, Indonesian, Japanese, Korean, Norwegian, Polish, Portuguese, Romanian, Russian, Slovak, Spanish, Swedish, and Thai.

For books and audiocassettes by Dr. McGinnis, or to inquire about Dr. McGinnis's availability for seminars, write or call Dickinson Publishing Group, 1110 Catalina Drive, Glendale, California, 91207, 818-247-7496, docmcginnis@msn.com.

Contents

Preface
to the Revised
Edition

WHEN DIANE AND I FOUND AN ADVANCE COPY of *The Friendship Factor* on our doorstep twenty-five years ago, we ripped open the package. We held the book at arms length to look at the cover together. We fondled it, thumbed through it, turned it over and over, made certain there was print inside, pulled it to our noses to take in the fragrance of the new binding. Then we looked up and down the street to see if some neighbors might be outside to whom we could show the book.

"How many copies would it have to sell for you to consider it a success?" Diane asked.

"Dunno. Never thought about it."

"Well think about it. For fun, pick a number."

I had heard somewhere that publishers break even on a book at about ten thousand copies. I was grateful to Augsburg for gambling on an unknown and unpublished writer, and didn't want them to lose money. So I said, "Honey, if it sold ten thousand copies I'd be so happy."

"Think it will?"

"Can't see how."

Now, twenty-five years later, without appearing on most best-seller lists, *The Friendship Factor* has sold close to two million copies, been translated into about twenty languages, and has continued to sell steadily year after year. Crazy things happen.

The publisher has asked me to comment on how one can account for this widespread distribution. I hesitate to offer opinions. I certainly am not under any illusion that the book is the psychological masterpiece of our time.

However, I do have some ideas on why the *topic* has had a broad appeal. One of the assumptions of the book is that friendship is the learning ground for all other relationships. If we can learn to be skilled at friendship, we will also be good at attracting the opposite sex, building efficient teams at work, getting along with our parents, rearing our children, and staying tight with our mates.

Second, this is the only book on this topic—as far as I know—to use Jesus as the model for learning to love. While doing the original research, I read the New Testament several times (and have done so once again while doing this revision), trying to understand the principles and techniques Jesus demonstrated in each of his encounters with people.

How is it that this has become a best-seller in such diverse places as Poland, Sweden, Mexico, South Africa, Japan, Korea, and Slovakia? That's easy. Love is a world-wide, cross-cultural, bridge-building phenomenon. Although we may express our affection in different ways (an appropriate statement of tenderness between friends in Italy, might be offensive in Sweden), and although our cultures will cause different difficulties in connecting, we all long to love and be loved.

In my work as a psychotherapist during these ensuing years, I have become more convinced than ever that a restoring and renewing power resides in friendship. If people availed themselves of the love available to them, many therapists like me could close up shop.

While teaching my clients how to improve their connections with people, I have also become more and more convinced that anyone—no matter how introverted, no matter how bungling in previous friendships—can learn the skills of love. It only requires the resolution to do so, plus a willingness to learn the principles that great friends and lovers have used for thousands of years.

This conviction has come not only from my work but also from my life. The power of love has almost overwhelmed me at times as I have continued to rub shoulders with the friends named in the first edition—most of all with Diane. But also with my children (now all adults), and with people such as Dr. Taz Kinney, Dr. John Todd, Dr. Neil Warren, and, until his death, Mr. Mark Svensson. (When Mark died at age eighty the two of us had by then been meeting for lunch at least once a week for thirty years.) What's more, in these twenty-five years a new crowd has decided to join our family. Christopher, Tyler, Avery, and Hope have brought the kind of laughter and love into their grandparents' home that only infants and little children provide. With such people I have done more than observe the power of friendship—I have felt it.

In this new anniversary edition, changes have been made on every page and it has been enlarged by three chapters. In particular, I have tried to include data from new psychological research on why friendships go awry. An explosion of studies in the last two decades has revealed much new data about the human brain and about why we feel the things we feel. With that has come an entire new genre of personal growth books written by bona fide experts on psychology and neurology, containing not mere advice and inspiration but lots of scientific data to substantiate the ideas. I am referring to Martin E. P. Seligman's *Learned Optimism* and *Authentic Happiness*, George Vaillant's three books of data gleaned from the Grant Study at Harvard, Edward Hollowell's *Connect*, and Daniel Goleman's *Emotional Intelligence*. I have been influenced by all seven of these books and others of their class. And have borrowed from them shamelessly.

When giving seminars on "How to Get Closer to the People You Care For" at churches I found that people were most interested in how to cope with negative emotions in friendships. Doubtless because Christians often feel guilty about those emotions. So I have expanded the sections on anger, taking into account new research on useful techniques for anger management. It turns out that I was wrong in some of my conclusions in the first edition. Potentially explosive situations can be handled in many ways, some of them better than the ones I suggested here originally. For instance, when certain types of people "ventilate" their anger, it doesn't bring relief at all. In fact, the anger seems to feed on itself, and the person gets more and more out of control. The old rule of counting to ten—which implied without the fancy terminology that it was useful to let the autonomic nerve system calm down so that it does not dictate our behavior—works.

One of the light bulbs to go off in my head during these twenty-five years is the discovery that our self-perception—a slippery phenomenon—has much more to do with our relationships than I initially realized. Hence the three new chapters on Identity and Intimacy.

ONE RESULT OF THE PUBLICATION OF *THE FRIENDSHIP Factor* for which I was quite unprepared was the number of invitations that came, asking for lectures at corporate meetings and trade associations. I had always done church conferences, but this was all new. Why would such groups want a speaker who knows nothing about business? Why would a book about relationships—with many references to the life of Jesus—be of interest to companies such as IBM, Metropolitan Life, and Robertson's Ready-Mix? As I met high-level executives of such companies at their meetings in many parts of the world, I learned the reason. They told me that human interactions were the single most difficult challenge they faced in their organizations—far more difficult than technological problems—and that if their employees could profit from studying friendship and relational patterns, with some help from the life of Christ, so much to the good. Those discussions led to another seminar, "Bringing Out the Best in People." That, in turn, led to a new book with that title. The people at Augsburg Fortress were good enough to publish it, and it now sells at a rate equal to this volume.

A NEW GENERATION IS TEACHING US A GREAT DEAL about friendship. If one listens carefully to rap and hip-hop music, it is, like music from the beginning of time, all about love, its power and its problems. Many members of this generation are the products of divorce and are determined not to repeat their parents' failures. I believe they will be quite successful. The revisions to this book have been written while listening to MTV and VH1 at times, and if it can offer some help to our young people in developing life-long commitments to others, it will have been worth sublimating my natural preference for Bach.

Young people today have added a splendid expression to our vocabulary. They talk about "hanging out." My generation thought that when we were with friends we had to be *doing* something—playing golf, having dinner, being entertained. But kids today have discovered that the best times can occur when people simply enjoy being in each other's company. You may or may not go anywhere. If you do, perhaps it's to put some gas in the car and pick up a video. But you do it together.

You may get together at someone's apartment and listen to music, but whether you are driving or sitting on the couch, you talk. Talk is at the heart of hanging out. Your best friends may be of the opposite sex without anything sexual in the mix; and when relationships do become romantic, that doesn't mean that the two of you stop spending many hours a week with your friends. Talking.

A life fully lived requires more than hanging out, of course. It requires some creative work, some service to people who do not have a supportive network. It should also, in my opinion, include spiritual aspirations that lead to a connection with God. Nevertheless, for my workaholic, stressed, and driven generation, hanging out is an antidote we need, and I thank this new crowd for the concept. Although the term did not exist then, it aptly describes much of what I originally tried to write about here years ago.

Enough preliminaries.

The aim of this book is to offer practical principles and techniques for getting closer to the people you care for, and chapter 1 lays the groundwork.

Loy McGinnis
Glendale, California
January 2004

Author's Notes

First Edition

Thanks to the following persons who have read pages from this book and made helpful suggestions: Jeff Hansen, Tricia Kinney, Dr. Lee Kliewer, Alan McGinnis Jr., Inez McGinnis, Dr. Walter Ray, Bob and Susan Ritchie, Ed Spangler, Dr. Bruce Thielemann, Dr. John Todd, and Karen Todd.

David Leek was the first to say, "This is publishable!" and Mike Somdal has taken a great interest in the project from the beginning.

Acknowledgment is made to Simon and Schuster for permission to quote from *How to Win Friends and Influence People* by Dale Carnegie and to Word Books for permission to quote from *No Longer Strangers* by Bruce Larson.

For the sake of privacy, all case histories from my counseling practice are composites, with names, places, and details sufficiently scrambled to make them unidentifiable. The shapes of the people's lives, however, are all true.

Second Edition

In the original typescript for the first edition, I expressed my appreciation and affection for Mr. Roland Sebolt, the editor-in-chief for books at what was then Augsburg Publishing House. Before the book went to press, however, he axed his name out, saying that the house had a firm rule against any mention of its staff in acknowledgments.

I was disappointed, because I owed Roland a great deal. Now, since he has long since retired, I have the liberty to give him credit.

It was Roland who had seen a short article in an obscure magazine that shortly thereafter folded. The article was titled "The Rich Rewards of Friendship." He somehow tracked me down in California, called, and said, "I think there's a book in that article."

"Funny thing, I've been working on one for several years," I replied. What I did not tell him was that the manuscript had been turned down by every major publisher in New York. Sometimes twice, because when it came back, I'd address it to another editor at the same company and try again.

I had almost given up. So when a small publisher from Minneapolis called *me* and wanted to see the book, I was delighted. Not only did Roland come to vigorously believe in the project, he also gave me astute advice on how to cast the material. Then it was he, who at the Frankfurt Book Fair each year, aggressively pushed it for translation in other languages. As we worked together on this and other projects, I came to regard him as one of the most loved and admired mentors I've ever had.

MR. RICHARD A. DICKINSON, WHO, IN ADDITION to being my wife's brother, is more like a brother to me than anyone, has been both gentle and generous in making suggestions for this edition.

Dedication, First Edition

PERHAPS A MAN LEARNS ALMOST AS MUCH ABOUT relationships when he fails at intimacy as when he succeeds. I have done both.

But this book is dedicated to the people who have been my teachers in success.

First, my colleagues, Taz Kinney, M.D., and Markus Svensson. We are in and out of each other's offices all day long, not merely because we need to discuss cases, but because we need to talk with one another about ourselves. I tell them my little victories and my large defeats. I can do this because they do the same with me.

And then there is the crew in the front office: Dagny Svensson, Katrina Grant, Monika Baaska, and Colleen Acord. Each means something different to me, and each is more than an administrative assistant.

Relationships have a way of being intergenerational. Looking in one direction, I owe all that I know about love to Alan and Inez McGinnis, from whose loins I came. Looking in the other direction, my children, Sharon, Alan, Scott, and Donna, are benefactors of the love another generation gave me, yet at the same time I learn of love from them.

But most of all, this book is for Diane, who tells me I am her best friend and who certainly is that to me. It is one of life's happiest gifts that we get to be married to each other.

Loy McGinnis
Glendale, California
January 1979

CHAPTER 1

The Rich Rewards of Friendship

Life is to be fortified by many friendships. To love, and be loved, is the greatest happiness of existence.
—Sydney Smith

HAVE YOU EVER WONDERED HOW CERTAIN PEOPLE are able to draw others to them and gain the admiration and affection of friends? Some men and women with average looks attract the opposite sex like iron shavings to a magnet. Executives who may not appear particularly brilliant sometimes move in an extensive network of loyal friends, and because of that they advance rapidly.

Such people may or may not be wealthy, witty, or buttressed with an expensive education. But somewhere in their personalities is an ingredient causing them to be respected and admired. It is what I call the friendship factor.

1

My work as a psychotherapist has furnished me with an unusual window on the interconnections of human beings. I have talked to thousands of people about their closest relationships, and in watching what the successful lovers do, I have learned some of their secrets. The aim of this book is to pass those secrets on to you.

How the Friendship Factor Can Make You an Expert at Intimacy

In research at our clinic, my colleagues and I have discovered that friendship is the springboard to every other love. Friendships spill over onto the other important relationships of life. People with no friends usually have a diminished capacity for sustaining *any* kind of love. They tend to go through a succession of marriages, be estranged from various family members, and have trouble getting along at work. On the other hand, those who learn how to love their friends tend to make long and fulfilling marriages, work well on business teams, and enjoy their children.

Soon after Jack Benny died, George Burns was interviewed on TV. "Jack and I had a wonderful friendship for nearly fifty-five years," Burns said. "Jack never walked out on me when I sang a song, and I never walked out on him when he played the violin. We laughed together, we played together, we worked together, we ate together. I suppose that for many of those years we talked every single day."

If we knew nothing else about those two, we could safely assume that they had solid relationships in other areas of their lives. Why? Because friendship is the model for all intimate encounters.

The basic ingredients for a good marriage, according to sociologist Andrew Greeley, are friendship plus sex.

And what about our relationships with our parents and our children? Henry Luce, founder of Time-Life, Inc., probably influenced world opinion more than any publisher in his time. His magazines circulated to more than thirteen million people, with international editions in two hundred countries. He not only constructed a financial empire; he also revolutionized modern journalism.

Luce frequently reminisced about his boyhood years as a missionary's son in Shantung, China. In the evenings he and his father had gone for long walks outside the compound, and his father had talked to him as if he were an adult. The problems of administering a school and the philosophical questions occupying his father were all grist for their conversational mill. "He treated me as if I were his equal," said Luce. Their bond was tight because they were friends, and both father and son were nourished by the relationship.

Why Women Have More Friends

"Are you close to anybody?" I asked. "Is there someone you can tell everything to, or almost everything?" She was a new client, reeling from a divorce, and I was trying to determine whether she was a candidate for psychotherapy.

"Oh, yes," she answered brightly. "I never would have made it through this mess without her. Actually, she's twenty-six years older than me, but we tell each other all our secrets. We're life-friends."

She is a fortunate woman, and we agreed at the end of the hour that as long as she had such a confidante, she didn't need a shrink.

Why are such friendships so rare among men? Conditioning, of course. In our society, except to shake hands, men are not even allowed to touch each other. Dick and Paula McDonald explain the phenomenon:

> Most men have had neither practice in the art of intimacy nor role models to point the way. Little girls can walk to school hand in hand, hold each other up skating, hug and cry and say, "You're my best friend. I need you. I love you." Little boys wouldn't dare.

And ultimately, of course, that affects their behavior toward the women they will meet.

Some of America's leading psychologists and therapists were asked how many men ever have real friends. The bleak replies were "not nearly enough" and "too few." Most guessed at 10 percent. Richard Farson, professor at the Humanistic Psychology Institute in San Francisco, says, "Millions of people in America have never had one minute in their whole lifetime where they could 'let down' and share with another person their deeper feelings."

Because so few males have been allowed the luxury of openness and vulnerability in a relationship, they are not aware of the gaping void in their emotional lives. In short, they don't know what they're missing.

In one study, British sociologist Marin Crawford found that middle-aged men and women had considerably different definitions of friendship. By an overwhelming margin, women talked about trust and confidentiality, while men described a friend as "someone I go out with" or "someone whose company I enjoy." For the most part, men's friendships revolve around activities while women's revolve around sharing. A man will describe as "my very good friend" a person who is an occasional tennis partner or someone he met a few days ago. But are they friends? Hardly.

As Paula McDonald makes clear, young women are newly aware of these issues and increasingly selective. "I think more women are looking for a sensitive man today," says Lynn Sherman, "and it really doesn't make any difference to us if he can lift up the couch with one hand or two. I think it's a responsive friend-type person most younger women want now."

It's OK to Be an Introvert

In my hometown an obscure nurseryman died some time ago. His name was Hubert Bales, and he was the shyest man I ever met. When he talked, he squirmed, blinked his eyes rapidly, and smiled nervously.

Hubert never ran in influential circles. He grew shrubs and trees, working with his hands the plot of land left to him by his father. He was anything but an extrovert.

Yet when Hubert died, his funeral was one of the largest in the history of our little town. There were so many people that they filled even the balcony of the church.

Why did such a shy man win the hearts of so many people? Simply because, for all his shyness,

Hubert knew how to make friends. He had mastered the principles of caring, and for more than sixty years he had put people first. Perhaps because they recognized that his generosity of spirit was an extra effort for someone so retiring, people loved him back. By the hundreds.

When I urge that you devote yourself to friendship, I am not urging you to become an extrovert. Some people suppose that their basic shyness is the problem.

One evening a neurosurgeon and I stood silently at the window, watching the lights of the city far below us. It was not easy for him to begin counseling—that was obvious from the way he nursed his coffee and felt me out with small talk. We had arranged this first meeting at night so he would not have to risk an encounter with any doctor friends in our elevators.

Finally, he took a deep breath, like a man about to dive into a cold swimming pool, and said:

"I guess I'm here because I'm messing up all my relationships. All these years I've fought to get to the top of my profession, thinking that when I got there people would respect me and want to be around me. But it hasn't happened."

He crushed the empty Styrofoam cup in his fist, as if to emphasize his desperation.

"Oh, I suppose I command some respect down at the hospital," he went on, "but I'm not close to anybody, really. I have no one to lean on. I'm not sure you can help me either—I've been shy and reserved all my life. What I need is to have my personality overhauled!"

How People Change

Had I met this man when I began counseling forty-five years ago—fresh from graduate school and very brash—I probably would have attempted the total overhaul he sought. But the longer I have worked with people the more reverence I have gained for the infinite complexity of the human personality. And the more reluctant I have become to try changing anyone.

One of the dangers of being a psychologist-reformer is that you may be tempted to try to remake all clients in your own image. But God made each of us unique, and there is vast mystery and beauty surrounding the human soul. Good psychotherapists are something like astronomers who spend their lives studying the stars, trying to determine why certain stellar systems behave as they do and why black holes exist. And at the end they are even more in awe of the grandeur of it all.

Although I will never understand my clients fully, my goal is to sit beside them as they search out themselves. The two of us will study the make-up and watch the movements of this person before us, seeking to understand the total system. It would be as presumptuous of me to attempt to overhaul that system as for an astronomer to remake the solar system. If I can help clients understand who God made them to be, and then help them to *be* those men and women, it is quite enough.

So I told my shy friend that I had no desire to change him into a garrulous and gregarious back-slapper. Besides, it was not so much his quiet personality as his patterns of relating that were getting him into trouble. When he exchanged those bad habits for some good relational skills, his life changed. He found himself talking more freely to his patients, and other doctors began to open up to him.

Today he is still an introvert. But he has three or four strong relationships, and the last time I saw him he was clearly a more fulfilled person.

You may or may not be the life of the party. If not, that will have little to do with your learning to love and be loved. In fact, as we will see later, you may be more capable of good relationships than the man who wears lampshades at the party and keeps them laughing all evening.

Friendship: A Valuable Commodity

Jesus placed great value on relationships. He chose to spend much of his time deepening his connections with a few significant persons rather than speaking to large crowds. What is more, his teaching was filled with practical suggestions on how to befriend people and how to relate to friends. The commandment on this topic was so important that he introduced it with an opening flag: "I give you a new commandment, that you love one another. Just as I have loved you, you also should love one another. By this everyone will know that you are my disciples, if you have love for one another" (John 13:34-35).

Those words are now two thousand years old, but their currency is demonstrated by a famous study. In his book *The Broken Heart*, Dr. James J. Lynch shows that lonely people live significantly shorter lives than the general population. Lynch, a specialist in psychosomatic disease, cites a wealth of statistics to demonstrate the unhealthy aspects of isolation and the magical powers of human contact.

Even viewed from a financial perspective, our friendships are our most valuable commodity. Studies many years ago at what was then the Carnegie Institute of Technology revealed that even in such fields as engineering, about 15 percent of one's financial success was due to one's technical knowledge and about 85 percent was due to skill in human engineering—to personality and the ability to lead people.

Dr. William Menninger estimated that when people are fired from their jobs, social incompetence accounts for 60 to 80 percent of the failures. Technical incompetence accounts for only 20 to 40 percent.

Your Past Failures at Love Need Not Be Repeated
"I have tried over and over," said a musician with a crew cut. "And I'd just as well accept it—I can't make it with people. I'm going to be alone for the rest of my life."

He had come to our office for an antidepressant medication. He didn't get any pills, but he did get some help with his relationships, and the depression disappeared in the process. My colleagues and I were able to help him forget his track record and concentrate on learning the art of friendship. While in therapy he could analyze his failures as they happened. When he was rejected he learned to pick himself up, profit from his mistake, and try love again. It did not come easily for him, but gradually he began to connect.

At the wedding of that musician, the delight in his bride's darting eyes confirmed that he had learned the art of love very well. His previous failures had not kept him an emotional cripple.

Abraham Lincoln considered himself to be a dismal flop with people in his early years. Proposing to Mary Owens in 1837, he added gloomily, "My opinion is that you had better not do it." And after Miss Owens turned him down, Lincoln wrote to a friend, "I have now come to the conclusion never again to think of marrying, and for this reason—I can never be satisfied with anyone who would be blockhead enough to have me."

Yet that man went on to master the art of dealing with people. When Lincoln drew his last breath, Secretary of War Stanton—once his livid enemy—said, "Now he belongs to the ages."

If we require further proof that we can learn to love and be loved, we can look at the life of Benjamin Franklin. As ambassador to France he was the most sought-after man in Paris. But was Franklin always this popular? Hardly. In his autobiography he describes himself as a blundering young man—uncouth and unattractive. In Philadelphia one day an old Quaker friend took young Franklin aside and said: "Ben, you are impossible. Your opinions have a slap in them for everyone who differs with you. They have become so expensive nobody cares for them. Your friends find they enjoy themselves better when you are not around."

One of the finest things we know about Franklin is the way he accepted that smarting rebuke. He was wise enough to realize that he was headed for failure and social disaster, and by applying himself to the laws of friendship, he turned himself around.

No One Has to Be Alone

You can learn the laws of relating as surely as Abraham Lincoln and Benjamin Franklin did. Each of the following chapters will give a simple rule for making your relationships work. These principles are not original with me. They have been distilled from the experiences of clients who have become my friends and from the writings of philosophers and psychologists ranging from Socrates to the latest neuropsychiatric researchers. Moreover, I have ransacked history books and read hundreds of biographies to determine what made the great historic friendships and love affairs work.

If you will set yourself the goal of mastering these techniques, you can become an expert at intimacy, for you can learn these skills as surely as you can learn to play the piano or program a computer.

I am not saying that these are easy skills to master; our connections with people are exceedingly complex. But they *can* be learned, and becoming an expert at friendship will be one of the most rewarding projects of your lifetime.

PART I

FIVE WAYS TO DEEPEN

YOUR RELATIONSHIPS

CHAPTER 2

Why Some People Never Lack Friends

Love must be learned,
and learned again and again;
there is no end to it.
Hate needs no instruction,
but wants only to be provoked.
   —Katherine Anne Porter

HE WAS THE WORLD'S ULTIMATE MYSTERY—SO secretive, reclusive, and enigmatic that for more than fifteen years no one could say for certain that he was alive, much less how he looked or behaved.

Howard Hughes was one of the richest men in the world, with the destinies of thousands of people—perhaps even of governments—at his disposal, yet he lived a sunless, joyless, half-lunatic life. In his later years he fled from one resort hotel to another—Las Vegas, Nicaragua, Acapulco—and his physical appearance became odder and odder. His straggly beard hung down to his waist and his hair reached to the middle of his back. His fingernails were two inches long, and his toenails hadn't been trimmed for so long they resembled corkscrews.

Hughes was married for thirteen years to Jean Peters, one of the most beautiful women in the world. But never in that time were the two seen in public together, and there is no record of their ever having been photographed together. For a while they occupied separate bungalows at the swank Beverly Hills Hotel, and later she lived in an opulent and carefully guarded French Regency house atop a hill in Bel Air, making secretive and increasingly infrequent trips to be with Hughes in Las Vegas.

They were divorced in 1970.

"As far as I know," a Hughes confidant once said, "he's never loved any woman. It's sex, or a good secretary, or good box office—that is all a woman means to him." Hughes often said, "Every man has his price or a guy like me couldn't exist," yet no amount of money bought the affection of his associates. Most of his employees who have broken the silence report their disgust for him.

Why was Hughes so isolated and so lonely? Why, with almost unlimited money, hundreds of aides, and countless beautiful women available to him, was he so unloved?

Simply because he chose to be.

It is an old axiom that God gave us things to use and people to enjoy. Hughes never learned to enjoy people. He was too busy manipulating them. His interests were machines, gadgets, technology, airplanes, and money—interests so consuming as to exclude relationships.

Love As a Priority

As I've watched those who are deeply loved, I've noticed they all regard people as a basic source of happiness. Their companions are very important to them, and no matter how busy their schedules, they have developed a lifestyle and a way of dispensing their time that allows them to have several profound relationships.

On the other hand, in talking to lonely persons I often discover that, though they lament their lack of close companions, they actually place little emphasis on the cultivation of friends. Like Howard Hughes, they are so occupied earning money, acquiring degrees, or building their stamp collections, that they do not have time to let love grow.

"We take care of our health," observed Emerson, "we lay up money, we make our rooms tight, and our clothing sufficient; but who provides wisely that he shall not be wanting in the best property of all—friends?"

So rule number one for deepening your friendships is:

Assign top priority to your relationships.

Loving and Losing

I am sometimes asked, "Dr. McGinnis, do you really think love is worth it?" Frequently the questioner has been divorced and is afraid that loving again will result in pain again. Others are reluctant to establish close friendships when they are so much on the move. After dozens of transfers, one wife of a highly mobile executive explained, "We've discovered that to prevent the pain of saying good-bye we no longer say hello."

Such persons have probably never known deep love, for anyone who has enjoyed intimacy and given any thought to it agrees with the poets who have been saying in various ways for centuries that love is always worth it. Upon the death of his friend, A. H. Hallam, Alfred Lord Tennyson famously declared, "'Tis better to have loved and lost than never to have loved at all."

I have had relationships that ended. In a few instances the failures have been rather spectacular, leaving a residue of emotional pain. But however brief the love's duration and however painful its terminus, I look back with gratitude.

If the termination occurred merely because the friend moved away, there is comfort in knowing that across the country someone knows me and cares about me.

My mother and father always lived in Texas, and I lived thousands of miles away from them all my adult life. Although they have long since died, I doubt that a day goes by without my thinking of them. When I was a boy they surrounded me with love, and when I grew up and struck out alone they continued to show an intense, benevolent interest in what I did, thought, and felt. So when my thoughts linger with them it brings me warmth—I am becalmed and given a sense of well-being simply because we loved one another.

Helen Keller once said, "With the death of every friend I love . . . a part of me has been buried . . .

but their contribution to my being of happiness, strength, and understanding remains to sustain me in an altered world."

Sixty years ago, a group of researchers began an ambitious, longitudinal study of 268 college students, who have been followed carefully since. These people, now in their 80s, varied in the success of their careers and also in overall life satisfaction. Some became corporation presidents, others stagnated in mid-life, and still others died as alcoholics or suicides. What configuration of traits, displayed at an early age, could predict success later in life? The researchers found, to their surprise, that school performance had almost no connection to future job competence, and that other qualities were more important. For instance, Dr. George E. Vaillant—the Harvard psychiatrist who has directed the study for several decades—looked closely at those who never found financial success or even reached middle management. *Not one had achieved intimacy, as reflected by stable marriages and lasting friendships.* "Contrary to common mythology," says Vaillant, "it was the very men who enjoyed the best marriages and richest friendship patterns who became the company presidents."

So much for the stereotype of an executive who is a star at the office but has no friends outside of work and is a flop at home.

One might argue that those who failed at friendship and marriage also failed at business for the same reason: lack of social skills. But it is probably more complicated than that. When you store up large quantities of love, and when you have friends and family to go home to after a stormy day at the office, love becomes a keel that pulls your ship back up. As always, there are exceptions, such as Howard Hughes. There will always be those who drive themselves in business to compensate for failures in other places. But in general, there is a direct correlation between the amount of love in your personal life, and the amount of success you have in the outside world.

Too Few and Too Many Friends

Dr. Stephen Johnson suggests asking yourself the following questions about your relationships:

• Do you have at least one person nearby whom you can call on in times of personal distress?

• Do you have several people whom you can visit with little or no advance warning?

• Do you have several people with whom you share recreational activities?

• Do you have friends who will lend you money, or those who will care for you in practical ways when the need arises?

If your responses to Johnson's questions are largely negative, it may be that your friendships are being impeded by your social life. Some people immerse themselves in such a whirl of parties and social affairs that there is no opportunity to establish a close relationship. The fact of the matter is that one cannot have a profound connection with more than a few people. Time prohibits it. Deep friendship requires cultivation over the years—evenings before the fire, long walks together, and lots of time for talk. It requires keeping the television off so that the two of you can log in with each other. If your social calendar is too full to provide for such intimate bonding, it should be pared. "True happiness," said Ben Jonson, "consists not in the multitude of friends, but in the worth and choice."

Some people get a strong sense of togetherness from being in large groups of people, and I am not arguing for or against an active social life. What I *am* lobbying for is an ordering of priorities. Getting close to a few people is more important than being popular enough to receive four hundred Christmas cards every year.

Love: The Road to Happiness

"The surest way to be miserable," said George Bernard Shaw, "is to have the leisure to wonder whether or not you are happy." We do not usually discover happiness in the pursuit of it. Most often it is a by-product, coming to us as we are in the midst of giving ourselves to another. Jesus said in several contexts and in several ways that we find ourselves by losing ourselves.

A young woman expressed the meaning of intimacy for her:

> With these friends you make a real effort, and then you break the barrier and you go beyond. This is a fantastic thing—you go home and lie awake because so many facts in your mind and soul have been opened. And when it is happening, I forget everything. It's not physical at all. I can sit with a drink of water, and I don't need cigarettes, wine, sex, food. It's a feeling of discovery, that something here inside you seems to be growing and

opening and expanding. And then the next day I am more energetic and optimistic. Going through the effort of sharing, of getting involved, was worthwhile. It is an increase of power, strength, energy.

Why do we seldom relate at such a level? Why is there such a shortage of close friendships? One simple reason: We do not devote ourselves sufficiently to it. If our relationships are the most valuable commodity we can own in this world, one would expect that men and women everywhere would be pursuing them with enthusiasm. But for many, it does not even occur in their list of goals. They apparently assume that love will "just happen."

But of course few of the valuable things in life "just happen." When they happen it is because we recognize their importance and devote ourselves to them. You can have almost anything you want if you want it badly enough. If you want to make a million dollars badly enough you probably can do it. If you want to run the Boston Marathon badly enough you probably can. And if you want love you can have that, too.

So rule number one is:

Assign top priority to your relationships.

CHAPTER 3

The Art of Self-Disclosure

Love consists in this, that two solitudes protect and touch and greet each other.
—Rainer Maria Rilke

PEOPLE WITH DEEP AND LASTING FRIENDSHIPS MAY be introverts, extroverts, young, old, dull, intelligent, homely, good-looking; but the one characteristic they always have in common is their lack of a facade. They have a certain transparency, allowing you to see what is in their hearts.

So rule number two for deepening your friendships is:

Cultivate transparency.

When Betty Ford became America's first lady, she soon became noted for her candor. When asked by pushy reporters her views on various topics, she gave them forthrightly. Once, when a newsman even went so far as to ask how often she slept with her husband, she replied, "As often as I can." Later, she did not try to withhold information about an earlier nervous breakdown or her battles with alcohol and drugs.

Those who possess Mrs. Ford's transparency are always able to have significant relationships. I am not saying that such openness will lead to universal popularity—Mrs. Ford incurred considerable ire from groups who did not appreciate her stand on certain issues. But if you are willing to be open, there will be people who cannot keep from loving you.

Pope John XXIII elicited warmth from people everywhere he went, in part because he completely lacked pretense. Fat all of his life, the son of a poor peasant family, he never pretended to be more than he was. After being elected Pope, one of his first acts of office was to visit Regina Coeli, a large jail in Rome. As he was giving the prisoners his blessing, he remarked that the last time he had been in jail was to visit his cousin!

Here was a man considered by millions to be Christ's vicar on earth, yet he knew how to share the hurts and joys of all people everywhere. As Conrad Barrs says, John XXIII was "maskless."

In his book *The Transparent Self,* psychologist Sidney Jourard relates some illuminating studies about the subject of self-disclosure. His major finding is that the human personality has a natural, built-in inclination to reveal itself. When that inclination is blocked and we close ourselves to others, we get into emotional difficulties.

Dr. Jourard stumbled onto this concept while puzzling over the frequency with which patients said to him: "You are the first person I have ever been completely honest with."

"I wondered," wrote Jourard, "whether there was some connection between their reluctance to be known by spouse, family, and friends, and their need to consult with a professional psychotherapist." His conclusion was that habitual dissembling and withdrawal leads to disintegration of the personality; and that, on the other hand, honesty literally can be a health insurance policy, preventing both mental illness and certain kinds of physical sickness.

However valid Dr. Jourard's theory about honesty promoting health, there can be no doubt that honesty promotes friendship. We like people who reveal themselves to us.

Masks

Why, then, do we so often hide behind masks? It is a conundrum—we vacillate between the impulse to reveal ourselves and the impulse to protect ourselves with a blanket of privacy. We long both to be known and to remain hidden.

We build walls around us for a number of reasons. Our culture seems to admire the cool hero like James Bond, who is tough, self-reliant, emotionally inexpressive, detached from personal involvement. And some—especially men—suppose that we will be liked if we can become similar rugged individualists who are always in control of every situation. Indeed, some *will* admire us for those qualities. But admiration does not necessarily lead to intimacy.

A more serious reason for our masks may be our fear of rejection. To take the step of self-disclosure and then have the person walk away can be devastating. Many of us have constructed elaborate facades because we are convinced that if people ever saw us as we see ourselves, the sight would repel them.

However, as I have watched clients in all kinds of interpersonal situations, I have found that self-disclosure has the opposite effect. When people take off their masks, others are drawn to them.

Some of us go to great lengths to hide our humble origins when honesty about them would disarm those around us and pull them into a more intimate connection.

The concert impresario, Sol Hurok, liked to say that Marian Anderson hadn't simply grown great, she'd grown great simply. He says:

> A few years ago a reporter interviewed Marian and asked her to name the greatest moment in her life. I was in her dressing room at the time and was curious to hear the answer. I knew she had many big moments to choose from. There was the night Toscanini told her that hers was the finest voice of the century. There was the private concert she gave at the White House for the Roosevelts and the King and Queen of England. She had received the Bok Award as the person who had done most for her hometown, Philadelphia. To top it all, there was that Easter Sunday in Washington when she stood beneath the Lincoln statue and sang for a

crowd of 75,000, which included Cabinet members, Supreme Court Justices, and most members of Congress.

Which of those big moments did she choose?

"None of them," said Hurok. "Miss Anderson told the reporter that the greatest moment of her life was the day she went home and told her mother she wouldn't have to take in washing anymore."

If we are open about our humble origins as well as our great moments, if we build more windows and fewer walls, we will have more friends.

One of the last barriers to come down as two people become more and more intimate is the wall of secrecy around their sexual feelings. One of the amazing discoveries I've made in my work is that a majority of married couples never discuss the topic. They have made love regularly for twenty-five years, but they've never talked about it. Often they do not even have the vocabulary for doing so. She may refer to his penis as his "thing," and he may not know what "clitoris" means. They never pronounce certain words in their partner's hearing.

But when we strip ourselves of our masks and allow ourselves to be known fully, the sexual experience can be immeasurably heightened. You invite the other to know your body and your mate offers you the same invitation. Sex ought to be an expression of the joy of life, a sharing of the good things in life. When sex is deeply enjoyed, freely given and taken, with deep, soul-shaking reactions from our bodies, it makes a well-married couple look at each other during breakfast with the children and wink and grin at each other.

In your nonsexual friendships, you can gauge the closeness by whether the two of you can talk freely about these matters. Only to intimates do we discuss sex. Among certain groups of men, of course, there is an obsession with the topic, but locker-room talk is mostly bragging and mostly fictional. I'm talking about the sort of friendship that is deep enough for you to describe not only your sexual ecstasies but also your sexual fears and uncertainties.

The best parent-child relationships must eventually accommodate this subject in their conversations, and the earlier you can become free enough to talk about sex with your children, the better your friendship can be.

A forty-three-year-old attorney had talked with me for almost a year about frustrations with his parents. They lived some distance away, but he longed to break down some of the barriers between him and his parents, especially his mother.

Then he flew home one weekend to tell his father and mother about the divorce that seemed to loom ahead for him. "I had no idea how they would take it," he said. "There had never been a divorce in my family, and I thought they might be pretty hard on me. But they weren't. They shed some tears, but they were supportive and sympathetic.

"However, the most important thing to happen that weekend occurred as Mom and I were sitting at the kitchen table after breakfast on Monday before I caught the plane home. Now to appreciate this story you need to know that my mom never pronounced the word s-e-x in the house as long as

I was growing up. What I learned about the topic I learned from books, friends, and mostly from girls.

"There I was, a grown man sitting with my mother, and she said, 'I'm so sorry things aren't working out for you and Shirley. I just wish that the two of you could have the kind of relationship your dad and I have. I never knew that sex could be so much fun for old folks.' Then she got a shy little twinkle in her eye and said, 'Of course, it's all because of your dad. He's always reading these books and thinking of new things to try.'"

The man's voice had a sense of awe as he related the conversation in my office the following week. He went on: "I can't explain it, but something clicked for me there at the kitchen table. I don't know whether it was because Mom and I were at last talking about an elemental drive very important to both of us, or whether it was because I felt good to know that my parents had such a good time in bed. Whatever it was, I've had an entirely new perspective on my mom since then."

James Joyce recognized that sometimes in the tiny moments of life light suddenly is shed on our whole existence. He might have called this man's experience an epiphany.

"I Feel Left Out of His Life"

"There must be more than this to live for," said the trim woman. "We've been married twenty-three years, but if there can't be something better ahead in our marriage, I think I'm ready to quit."

Her husband was a quiet man who kept his own counsel and took some pride in being calm in every situation. But his wife saw this as no virtue.

"I never know what he's thinking," she complained, "and I feel left out of his life."

Very often a therapist knows such a husband only through his mate's eyes, for he is by nature very afraid of the probing of therapy and would never come near a counselor's office. But in this case the story has a happy ending. Joel was willing to give marriage therapy a try, and it turned out— as it often does—that his protective walls hid a multitude of fears, phobias, and insecurities. He had been afraid to talk about these aspects of himself for fear that his wife would look down on him when she knew how weak he was. The irony was that she was on the verge of leaving him pre- cisely because of his protective walls. But when he began to reveal his insecurities, she knew better what was weighing on his mind and realized how he needed her. After that it was easy to feel tender toward him again.

You and Your Shadow Side

The brilliant Swiss psychiatrist Carl Jung advised his patients to become acquainted with what he called the "shadow side" of themselves. Indeed, there is a hidden section of the mind containing both memories from the past that terrify us, and certain mean, selfish, and base impulses that erupt occasionally. That part of our interiors we try to excuse and explain away in many ways. Especially to ourselves.

We will be very reluctant to reveal this side of ourselves to another so long as it scares us. But generally, others are able to be more lenient with us than we are with ourselves. And a curious kind of chemistry begins to work. Because we have told another our deepest secrets, we begin to understand ourselves better.

I think I can even go as far as to say that you can never genuinely know yourself except as an outcome of disclosing yourself to another. When you reveal yourself to another person, you learn how to increase contact with your soul. Then you will be more able to direct your destiny on the basis of this knowledge. The Delphic oracle advised, "Know thyself," but we could expand that counsel: "Make yourself known, and you will then know yourself."

The Christian practice of confession has always been recognized for its therapeutic effect. The Bible advises: "Confess your sins to one another, and pray for one another, so that you may be healed" (James 5:16). It is not by accident that the biblical author says that if we acknowledge our dark side we will become whole. In ways we do not fully understand, self-disclosure helps us to see things, feel things, imagine things, hope for things that we could never have thought possible. The invitation to transparency, then, is really an invitation to authenticity.

Why We Are Drawn to Transparent People

Dr. Bruce Larson frequently advocated that we have at least one other person to whom we can tell everything. I was disturbed by his remark when I first read it, for I had never confided completely in anyone. I was willing to dole out bits and pieces to many people—some of it quite intimate material—but to attempt total disclosure to a single friend would be a huge leap.

However, a few years later I took that leap—or rather a friend, Markus Svensson—took that leap with *me*, emboldening me to do the same, and after that I knew the astonishing sense of security and comfort that washes over you when someone understands you fully, and continues to accept you fully. When Mark died three years ago, I was glad for his sake that he could shed his pain, but was bereft for myself. Mark and I had many differences. He was fifteen years older than I. He was short with a black beard; I am tall and blond. He was a skilled manufacturing executive who did not bother long with formal education; I have spent half my lifetime going to school. He was an immigrant from Sweden; I am a native Texan.

Yet I could be totally myself with Mark. He wasn't bothered by whatever vagaries of mood I brought, and I did the same with him. He did not always approve of my behavior or my thoughts, but I knew that he would not try to censure me. However angry we sometimes were with each other, our anger never shook the friendship.

Marian Evans (who used the pen name George Eliot) must have had such a friendship to have written:

> Oh the comfort, the inexpressible comfort of feeling safe with a person; having neither to weigh thoughts nor measure words but to pour them all out, just as it is, chaff and grain together, knowing that a faithful hand will take and sift them, keeping what is worth keeping, and then, with the breath of kindness blow the rest away.

A Surefire Way to Draw People Close

A famous psychiatrist was leading a symposium on methods of getting patients to open themselves. The psychiatrist challenged his colleagues with a blatant boast: "I'll wager that my technique will enable me to get a new patient to talk about the most private things during the first session without my having to ask a question." What was his magic formula? Simply this: He began the session by revealing to the patient something personal about himself—a secret with which the patient might damage the doctor by breaking the confidence. However questionable we may regard the doctor's manipulation, it had its desired effect: It released the patient to talk.

The same principle applies to all human relationships. If you will dare to take the initiative in self-revelation, the other person is much more likely to reveal secrets to you. There is no substitute for transparency in drawing out the beloved.

My mentor—the psychotherapist whom I would most like to emulate—was a man whom I never met. Yet I think I know him and his work intimately through his many books. They are not brilliant books on theoretical psychology. I read them not for their brilliance, but to absorb the gentle spirit with which he discusses his work with his clients. A simple and unpretentious man, Dr. Paul Tournier obviously had a great gift for healing. What was his secret?

He points to a significant turning point in his career. While practicing as an internist in Geneva, he attended a small meeting in a home where people were simply being themselves, sharing deeply of hurts, joys, sins, excesses. Although he had been a religious man before, Tournier says that in this climate he was spiritually transformed. When he returned to his medical practice, he found people opening up to him. Instead of talking only about their physical symptoms, patients began to talk about their lives. They opened themselves to him because he had become a transparent person himself, and openness elicits openness. Eventually Tournier restricted his practice to psychotherapy.

One of the most winsome and distinctive aspects of the life of Jesus was his remarkable transparency. Unlike most gurus who have remained aloof from their disciples, he lived out his life squarely in their midst. Breaking bread with them, weeping with them, helping them resolve their quarrels, praying for them, he was intensely involved in their common life. Again and again he opened himself to them, and when they did not understand him, he was grieved. To be sure that the disciples understood this deliberate self-disclosure, he told them: "I do not call you servants any longer, because the servant does not know what the master is doing; but I have called you friends, because I have made known to you everything that I have heard from my Father" (John 15:15). Transparency with one another, our Lord seems to be saying, signals that two acquaintances have become friends.

When we encounter people who are that transparent we are quickly stripped of our defenses. The Samaritan woman who met Christ at the Sychar well parried and sparred with him at first, wary because he was a stranger. But soon she stopped dissembling and, with an almost visible sigh of relief, she basked in the freedom of being known.

No one really likes wearing a mask. To be known and accepted by God is a liberating and healing experience, and it is the best model of all for our human relationships.

Total Honesty?

It is time to add a disclaimer or two, to make clear what I do *not* mean by transparency.

In the first place, I am not advocating that we be argumentative. Some who try to be "totally honest" give you their opinion on any subject you raise. If you venture an idea that does not square with theirs, "openness" requires that they disagree on the spot.

That is a foolhardy way to live. It is sometimes the part of prudence as well as courtesy to keep our opinion to ourselves.

In the second place, I am certainly not urging that we allow our emotional life to be an open book everywhere we go. Those who think psychological nudity a virtue may be more out of control than they realize, for one of the marks of severe psychosis is an inability to edit anything that comes into one's mind.

Most of us flee from men and women who tell us their entire life stories with intimate details in the first hour of acquaintance. It is unreasonable to attempt full disclosure with everyone, or even with *any* person at one sitting. All of us have the right to silence and must decide how much of ourselves to reveal at any given time.

One final caveat: We will want to exercise caution in revealing feelings or facts that may damage others or hurt the hearer. I am thinking specifically about the confession of sexual infidelity to your mate. Some therapists urge couples to cough up all old misdeeds, no matter how damaging the revelations. But in some cases, they are trying to relieve personal guilt, unaware that they have simply transferred the burden to the beloved's shoulders. Certain marriages have benefited from the catharsis of mutual confession and such a cleansing can sometimes draw the couple considerably closer. But confession does not always have such a salutary effect, and I am urging that it be done with great deliberation.

Our overriding principle, however, still stands. If you want to deepen your friendships, rule number two is:

Cultivate transparency.

CHAPTER 4

How to Communicate Warmth

Our opinion of people depends less upon what we see in them than upon what they make us see in ourselves.

—Sara Grand

ON 9-11-01, HUNDREDS OF PEOPLE WHO WERE not killed by the initial impact at the World Trade Center were trapped, but they still had access to cell phones. Others were passengers on what they knew to be a doomed flight over Pennsylvania. What was the message repeated again and again from those who were able to make connections with home? Was it directions about where to find wills or life insurance papers? Did they tell their husbands and wives what to do about selling the houses? No, those were the last things on their minds. Instead, they said again and again, "Honey, remember I love you," or "Please tell the kids over and over how much I love them." And if there was time, some said, "Please call Mom and tell her I love her."

When one distills the essence of our existence, it has almost nothing to do with houses or bank accounts or business achievements. It is all about love. And for a variety of reasons, we declare our love too infrequently—if at all—to many of the people we care for.

When Gale Sayers and Brian Piccolo, both running backs for the Chicago Bears, began rooming together in 1967, it was a first for race relations in professional football. It was also a first for both of them. Sayers had never had a close friendship with a white person before, with the possible exception of George Halas, and Piccolo had never *known* an African-American.

One secret of their growing friendship lay in their similar tastes in humor. Before the 1969 exhibition game in Washington, for instance, an earnest young reporter entered their hotel room for an interview.

"How do you two get along?" the writer asked.

"We're okay as long as he doesn't use the bathroom," said Piccolo.

"What do you fellows talk about?" asked the businesslike reporter, ignoring the guffaws.

"Mostly race relations," Gale said.

"Nothing but the normal racist stuff," Piccolo added.

"If you had your choice," the writer went on, "who would you want as your roommate?"

Sayers replied, "If you are asking me what white Italian fullback from Wake Forest, I'd have to say Pick."

But submerged beneath the horse laughs and the digs lay a fierce loyalty to each other, and as the movie "Brian's Song" poignantly depicted, the friendship between Sayers and Piccolo deepened into one of the best relationships in the history of sports.

Then, during the 1969 season, Piccolo was cut down with cancer. He fought to play the season out, but he was in the hospitals more than he was in the games. Gale Sayers flew to be beside him as often as possible.

They had planned, with their wives, to sit together at the Professional Football Writers annual dinner in New York, where Sayers was to be given the George S. Halas Award as the most courageous player in pro football. But instead Pick was confined to his bed at home. As he stood to receive the award, tears sprang to Sayer's eyes. The ordinarily laconic athlete had this to say as he took the trophy:

> You flatter me by giving me this award, but I tell you here and now that I accept it for Brian Piccolo. Brian Piccolo is the man of courage who should receive the George S. Halas Award. I love Brian Piccolo and I'd like you to love him. Tonight, when you hit your knees, please ask God to love him too.

I love Brian Piccolo. How much more enriched our lives could be if we dared to declare our affection as Sayers did that night in New York.

Rule number three for deepening your friend-ships is:

Dare to talk about your affection.

For fear of seeming sentimental, many of us hold back expressions of warmth and thereby miss out on rich and profound friendships. We say "thanks" when we mean "God bless you," and "so long" when we mean, "I'll miss you a lot." G. K. Chesterton once said that the meanest fear is the fear of sentimentality. It would add immeasurably to the amount of love abroad if we would be freer in declaring our affection. Jesus had a way of doing that. He said in a hundred different ways that he loved his disciples. There could have been no doubt in their minds of his affection.

Why are we so reluctant to say openly that we care for another? Several reasons. There is the pos-sibility that our overture of warmth will not be reciprocated and we will be rejected. Or even worse, especially among men, we are afraid of being laughed at for our sentimentality. There are few emotions more frightening than embarrass-ment, and we go to great lengths to avoid even the possibility of it.

But those who are loved widely are usually those who throw caution to the winds and declare their love freely. Thomas Jefferson, for instance, was a man's man, and he was more sensitive to rejection than most. At one point in his career, stung by Hamilton's victory over him in Washington, he shipped his books and furniture home to Monticello, cancelled his newspaper subscriptions, cut off his political contacts, and during the next thirty-seven months never stirred more than seven miles from home. Jefferson was that sensitive to ridicule.

Yet did his fear of embarrassment keep him from expressing his love when he felt it? Fawn M. Brodie, a Jefferson biographer, says: "His letters to his two adult daughters, Martha and Maria, are so affectionate and so innocently seductive that they become an open window." And writing to his cherished friend, John Adams, he could say in 1819 such "sentimental" things as: "Take care of your health and be assured that you are most dear to me."

Although Lafayette and Jefferson corresponded prolifically, they had not seen each other in thirty-five years when President Monroe invited the great French general to visit America in 1824. Lafayette was sixty-seven and Jefferson was eighty-one. Spending only one day in Quincy, Massachusetts, upon his arrival, Lafayette hurried south to see Jefferson.

On the November morning that Lafayette's carriage arrived at Monticello, a crowd had assembled to witness the meeting. John Randolf, who helped with the celebration, described how his grandfather walked down his terrace as Lafayette descended from the carriage. Jefferson, he said, "got into a shuffling quickened gait until they threw themselves with tears into each other's arms."

In working with divorced people I often wish they could take a lesson from people like Gale Sayers, Thomas Jefferson, and Jesus—people who have dared to declare their love. Many a single woman thinks she must play it cool on dates or risk driving men away. Although she may be attracted to him, she keeps her feelings to herself. But such aloofness actually defeats her purpose. There is nothing that will turn a man on more than knowing that a woman is attracted to him.

It is sad when two people come together and like what they see in each other, yet, because both are shy, they do not declare their affection and so the relationship sputters and dies. The tragedy is that the love goes unrequited simply because it is undeclared.

The Hard-to-Get Woman

If the above is true, then what are we to make of the age-long attraction to the aloof and distant woman? According to folklore, the woman who is hard to get is a more desirable catch than the woman who is overly eager for alliance. Socrates, Ovid, the *Kama Sutra,* and Dear Abby all agree on this.

But Dr. Elaine Walster and other researchers told in *Psychology Today* about an experiment with several hundred college men to determine their reaction to various women. When interviewed initially, the men said they preferred the hard-to-get woman because she could be choosy only if she were popular. And a woman is popular for some good reason. They said such women are usually more personable, pretty, and sexy—a combination hard to beat. They were intrigued by the challenge of the distant woman.

On the other hand, college men said that easy women spelled trouble. They were usually desperate for dates, and when they did get a man they became too serious, too dependent, and too demanding. In short, nearly all men interviewed agreed with the researcher's premise that it is smart for a woman to play it cool.

But the data broke down when the men were interviewed about their first dates, set up by computer, with women who were actually confederates of the experimenters. With half the men, the women were instructed to be aloof and elusive. With the other half, the confederates played friendly and affectionate almost immediately. The researchers had predicted that the women most in demand for a second date would be those who were choosy and proved to be a challenge. But just the opposite turned out to be true. The more romantic interest the girl displayed, the more desirable the male students judged her to be. Apparently, all the world *does* love a lover.

So back to the drawing board. The psychologists by this time were quite exasperated, so they scrapped their earlier hypotheses and returned to interviewing college men. This time they questioned each more carefully and asked them to tell about the advantages *and* disadvantages of the hard-to-get and easy-to-get women. They learned that both women were uniquely desirable and uniquely frightening. Although the elusive woman is likely to be a popular and prestigious date, she presents problems. Because she isn't particularly enthusiastic about you, she may stand you up or humiliate you in front of your friends. She's also likely to be unfriendly, cold, and inflexible—qualities a young man can certainly do without. On the other hand, even though the easy-to-get woman may become serious about you and hard to get rid of, she will boost your ego and make a date relaxing and enjoyable. The researchers began to conclude that the assets and liabilities of the two types balanced out.

Now came the conclusions from the study. They discovered that *if a woman has a reputation for being hard to get, but for some reason is easy for the subject to get, she is highly appealing.* Such a woman is dynamite for a man because she has the high appeal of being a woman who is selective, but when she meets a man she likes she does not hold back in declaring her feelings. Hence his dates with her are highly rewarding and enjoyable. The advice of those who conducted this study, then, is this: Be *selectively* elusive. If you embody the popularity and desirability of the distant woman but reach out with friendliness and warmth when you care for a man, you'll be a winner.

How to Generate an Emotional Field

Would you like a way of making another care for you that will work 90 percent of the time? It is so simple that I am almost embarrassed to say it. However, I know so many people who long to be loved and who do not practice this almost infallible rule that I will state it here. It is not original with me. Seneca expressed it succinctly almost two thousand years ago: "If you wish to be loved, love."

Those persons who will let their hearts go and who will freely declare their admiration and affection are very hard to turn down.

In his book *Love and Will,* Rollo May has a fascinating passage on this topic. It is so significant that I wish to quote it in full:

> [There is a] strange phenomenon in psy-
> chotherapy that when the patient feels some
> emotion—eroticism, anger, alienation, or hos-
> tility—the therapist normally finds himself
> feeling that same emotion. This inheres in the
> fact that when a relationship is genuine, they
> empathetically share a common field of emo-
> tion. This leads to the fact that, in everyday
> life, we normally tend to fall in love with those
> who love us. The meaning of "wooing" and
> "winning" a person is to be found here. The
> great "pull" to love someone comes precisely
> from his or her loving you. Passion arouses an
> answering passion.

So far as I know, Rollo May is the first to discuss
such a "field of emotion," yet all of us have experi-
enced a similar magnetic attraction to another and
the description is very apt. When people care for us
and show that appreciation with their eyes, their
attention, and their declarations of affection, we
find a certain passion generated. As May says, "The
great 'pull' to love someone comes precisely from
his or her loving you."

In Defense of Passion

Do you find yourself embarrassed to tell another
that you care? Let's look at some examples of passionate feelings expressed by experts.

"How I long for your presence, my darling."
That is Woodrow Wilson writing to his fiancée,
Ellen Axson in 1884. He goes on to express more of
what we might consider sentimental overstate-
ment: "It would be such a comfort and such pure

delight to sit in sweet communion with you at such times; to talk of the future, of how we shall sustain each other in love, of how we shall work together to do good, to make a bright spot around us in the world." Sentimental? Perhaps. But passion won the woman, as it has done for centuries.

Of course, sentimentalism can reach extremes. An apocryphal story, but one favored by romantics, concerns Restoration playwright Thomas Otway. He is said to have starved himself for three days, hoping to soften the heart of actress Elizabeth Barry, and then run into the street so hungry that he ate a loaf of bread too rapidly and choked to death.

If anyone was an expert at passion, it was Theodore Roosevelt. While a Harvard junior he met Alice Hathaway, the seventeen-year-old cousin of his best friend. At first sight he plunged dizzily in love; as his letters and diaries exuberantly testify, the passion was not merely for show. The diary entry for January 25, 1880, reads:

> A year ago last Thanksgiving I made a vow that win her I would if it were possible. And now that I have done so, the aim of my whole life shall be to make her happy. . . . And oh, how I shall cherish my sweet queen! How she, so pure and sweet and beautiful, can think of marrying me, I cannot understand, but I praise and thank God it is so.

Finally, one more. Marian Evans wrote in 1875 to Mrs. Burns-Jones:

I like not only to be loved, but also to be told
that I am loved. I am not sure that you are of
the same kind. But the realm of silence is large
enough beyond the grave. This is the world of
literature and speech, and I shall take leave to
tell you that you are very dear.

Who, receiving a letter like that, could be indifferent to its author?

Some Traps in Saying "I Love You"

There are pitfalls to avoid in the declaration of
love. The following people misuse the privilege:

The Gusher: This is the person whose mouth
spouts affectionate phrases every time it opens. If
you gush inappropriate and artificial emotion,
people will soon begin to discount everything you
say. Don't express anything you don't feel, but do
express every good feeling you have about others.

The Pressurizer: Here is the person who says "I
love you" in order to hear it back. Do not ask for a
compliment in return when you praise someone,
and do not ask for a commitment when you tell
another of your affection. Instead of a lever for
applying pressure, let your compliment be the free
expression of what is going on inside you.

The Ramrod: This is the deliverer of passionate
lines who is insensitive to the reaction of the other.
Dr. Stephen Johnson says that the process of getting closer to another person follows a one-two-three rule: First, reach out; second, notice the reaction; third, move forward, stop, or back up,
depending on the signals you receive.

The Tragedy of Waiting Until It's Too Late

Hugh was a young salesman with a head of curly hair and a strong handshake. He had come to my consulting room because he was muddled and confused about his career, and that was making him impotent. I asked about his childhood. Was it happy?

"Well, not really," he answered. "My father was gruff and always critical. I tried hard to please him when I was little, but he couldn't seem to bring himself to say anything good about me. Years after he died I was visiting my mother and went down to the tavern where Dad hung out. Some of his old cronies were there, and they related some very complimentary things my father used to say about me down at the factory. I was flabbergasted. I had no idea he felt that way."

I submit that is a tragic story. Such misunderstandings could be averted if people would dare to declare their affection as soon as they feel it. There is magic in the statement, "I love you." Your children will respond to it, your parents will be moved by it, your friends will love you for saying it.

Perhaps the words "I love you" will be too hard for certain men to say to each other, but there are other ways you can express your warm feelings. You can tell your friend that you've missed seeing him and that it means a lot to get together for lunch, or you can tell him that your friendship is one of the best things you own.

Sometimes you can double the return on the compliment by relaying it through another. If you tell a man's wife, for instance, how much you appreciate him, you make two people feel good:

her, because she likes other people to like her husband, and him, because you can be sure that she will tell him as soon as she gets home.

What I have been trying to say in this chapter Ben Franklin expressed in a single sentence: "Speak ill of no man, but speak all the good you know of everybody."

So rule number three for deepening your friendships is:

Dare to talk about your affection.

CHAPTER 5

Love Is Something You Do

That best portion of a good man's life—His little, nameless, unremembered, acts of kindness and love.
—William Wordsworth

FREDERICK SPEAKMAN ONCE WROTE A BOOK TITLED *Love Is Something You Do.* The title is apt, for when we think of love we tend to think of spectacular emotions and heroic acts. But little of life is passed in such moments of intensity, important as they are. The best friendships are built up, like a fine lacquer finish, with the accumulated layers of many acts of kindness.

When Albert Einstein's wife died in 1936, his sister Maja moved in to assist the great genius with his household affairs. In 1950 she suffered a stroke and lapsed into a coma. Thereafter, Einstein spent two hours each afternoon with her, reading aloud from Plato. Although she gave no sign of under-standing, his intuition told him that a part of her mind lived, and he knew how much love could be communicated through an attentive act.

Rule number four for improving your rela-tionships:

Learn the gestures of love.

In my work as a marriage counselor, I am fre-quently surprised at the naiveté of couples who become disillusioned when the first blush of romantic emotion has faded. With terrible guilt a woman will say, "Doctor, I'm afraid I don't love my husband anymore. What's wrong with me? When we got married I thought I loved him, and now sometimes I don't even *like* him." Nothing is wrong with her, of course, except that she is probably spending too much time analyzing her feelings.

The experts at love realize that emotions ebb and flow, and they look for gestures of love even when their emotions are on the wane. What's more, they are never content with telling the beloved they care—they show it in small expres-sions of affection. Mark Twain once said, "Love seems the swiftest, but it is the slowest of all growths."

A husband takes a long lunch hour and drives twenty miles home to take his wife to her favorite restaurant. A man sees a new book in the shop, buys it, and mails it to his friend's office with a note. A woman hears an acquaintance say she could eat watercress every day of her life, and she never has her for dinner without having watercress especially for her plate. These are the gestures that bond people together and prevent fractures when the relationship is under strain.

I talked to a man whose marriage had gone bad after eighteen years.

"How did you know it was over?" I asked.

"When she stopped putting toothpaste on my brush in the mornings," he replied.

"What?" I said.

"Well, when we were first married, whoever got up first would roll toothpaste on the other's brush and leave it lying on the sink. Somewhere along the line we stopped doing that for each other, and the marriage went downhill from there."

That, of course, is an oversimplification of why a marriage disintegrated, but the little courtesies do count. They count a lot.

"The roots of the deepest love," wrote von Herder, "die in the heart if not tenderly cherished," and Edna St. Vincent Millay lamented:

'Tis not love's going hurts my days,
But that it went in little ways.

The minuscule act of kindness has great power because it demonstrates that you have not taken your beloved for granted. You took the time to think what might bring a moment of happiness. Gelett Burgess sent a friend a book, which the friend promptly acknowledged. But two months afterward the woman wrote another letter, telling what she thought of the book, proving she had read it. "She had the educated heart," Burgess writes, "for to such persons thanks are something like mortgages, to be paid in installments."

The Significance of Rituals

Robert Brain, an anthropologist who studied friendship in several widely different cultures, said that ritual is one of the universally important ingredients in good relationships. When we stop to think about it, husbands and wives cement their love with many ceremonies: kissing good-night, celebrating anniversaries, giving jewelry, telephoning when they are apart, bringing each other breakfast in bed, taking an evening walk together.

The person sensitive to the deepening of friendship will be on the lookout for similar rituals. A weekly lunch together, a regular golf date, or a yearly fishing trip can be important events. Handshakes, hugs, joking and roughhousing—all these gestures put love in the bank and gain interest for the future.

When my son was in junior high I began driving him to school each morning, and it became our habit to eat breakfast together on the way. We tried several eateries until we found Vern's, where they served the perfect grilled English muffin. Sometimes we hardly talked over our eggs. At other times we revealed to each other profound emotions that we disclosed to no one else. That breakfast ritual helped us through the stormy adolescent years. My son is a grown man now and lives in another city, but when he comes home the family understands that the two of us must repair to Vern's at least one morning during his stay. It is a ritual of unspoken significance, which has accrued during the years.

One of the best ways to deepen a friendship is by eating together. It is no accident that so many important encounters occurred between Jesus and his friends when they were at the table. There is something almost sacramental about breaking bread with another and it is almost impossible to have dinner with an enemy and remain enemies.

So if you want to change an enemy into a friend, try inviting the person to your home and, with your feet under the same table, talk out the problem. Or if you wish to promote stronger relationships with more people, invite someone different to lunch every week or offer to meet people for coffee before work.

Another method of accumulating good memories is to help your friend with some task. Working shoulder-to-shoulder with another can tighten your relationship, even when few words are spoken. Look for the person who is doing some unpleasant task and offer to help get it done in half the time. You may be surprised at the warmth that will return to you in the future.

Married couples could enjoy each other more if they worked together more. Our foolish division of labor according to roles often leaves a wife indoors to wash the dishes while her husband goes outdoors to wash the car. Why not do both tasks together and enjoy each other's company in the process?

Part of the richness one feels in the best relationships is the result of many memories garnered over the years. Memories of favors done back and forth, tools lent, errands done, articles clipped for the other to read—a thousand tiny statements of love.

The Art of Giving Gifts

There is an art to one of the oldest gestures of love—the giving of gifts. The most lavish gift does not necessarily bespeak the most love. More important is the thoughtfulness the gift represents.

My wife's mind is always on the prowl to discover people's little preferences, and that quality makes her the best gift-giver I have ever known. The pen with which I am writing this chapter cost less than a dollar, yet it is one of her innumerable little presents that has delighted me. She overheard me saying that I liked the way a borrowed felt-tip pen wrote but I couldn't find the brand in any store. So she began shopping. A few days later I found on my desk a reminder of the way she thinks of me often during her waking day.

Exchanging gifts is an important gesture even among animals. Empidae, for instance—the common, minute flies that dance in clouds in the heavy summer air—have an elaborate courtship ritual. When the male goes courting he makes a selection of choice food dainties, wraps them in a shimmering quicksilver bubble of silk, and presents them to his desired partner.

Adelie penguins of the Antarctic do not have much choice in selecting love gifts in their barren land. But the male penguin searches among the stones and pebbles until he finds a smooth one, and then he waddles to his lady and lays that humble treasure at her feet.

Dr. Lars Granberg, who later went on to become a college president, was a struggling graduate student in Chicago during the first years of his marriage. His wife worked hard at her job to support the two of them. Granberg says:

> It was tough on my pride to be so poor and to have my wife working to put me through school, but I hit on a little investment that made me feel better. At one of the elevated railway stops on my way home at night, an old Italian florist had a small shop. I got off the train there for a minute every evening and bought a rose. The old man began to look for me and would have the flower ready so that sometimes I could hop off the train, grab the rose, and get back on before it pulled away. When I came in the door at night with my briefcase in one hand and that flower in the other, my wife would throw her arms around me and tell me how that meant more to her than three dozen bouquets.

Merle Simpson once told of being hospitalized when a friend and his five-year-old son came to visit. As soon as they entered the room, the boy lay three presents on the bed tray. They were toy cars with the paint worn off from hours of play.

"I started to refuse his gifts," says Simpson, "but I saw from the expression on his face that to do so would hurt my young friend. They were his precious possessions, and they told of his affection for me. That was many years ago and the boy now has children of his own. But I cherish those toys still."

The Ripple Effect of Kindness

Some acts of kindness spread out far beyond the original point of contact. Norman M. Lobsenz tells of a time when his young wife became desperately ill and he wondered how he would be able to cope with the physical and emotional burdens of caring for her. One evening, when he was drained of strength and endurance, a long-forgotten incident came to his mind:

> I was about ten years old at the time, and my mother was seriously ill. I got up in the middle of the night to get a drink of water. As I passed my parents' bedroom, I saw the light on. I looked inside. My father was sitting in a chair in his bathrobe next to Mother's bed, doing nothing. She was asleep. I rushed into the room.
>
> "What's wrong?" I cried. "Why aren't you asleep?"
>
> Dad soothed me. "Nothing's wrong. I'm just watching over her."

Lobsenz, without knowing exactly how, found the strength to take up his own burden again when he recalled that incident from long ago.

> The remembered light and warmth from my parents' room were curiously powerful, and my father's words haunted me: "I'm just watching over her." The role I now assumed seemed somehow more bearable, as if a resource had been called from the past, or from within.

When Kindliness Becomes a Habit

Someone has said that the test of great men and women is the way they treat little people, and if one can develop the habit of looking for gestures that build goodwill, kindliness can become second nature.

Birch Foracker was a top executive for the New York Bell Telephone Company. He had a reputation for walking out of the theatre on a cold night and leaving his party watching incredulously from the sidewalk as he crawled down into a manhole in the middle of the street. Why? To make sure that the crew working down there was all right on a winter's night, and to express his appreciation for their work. Acts such as that may not take more than sixty seconds, but they make a person greatly beloved.

"It is insufficiently considered how much of human life passes in little incidents," Samuel Johnson wrote in one of his essays. Our lives are shaped and directed by the accumulation of many common events, so rule number four for improving your relationships is:

Learn the gestures of love.

CHAPTER 6

Neglect This and Watch Your Friends Flee

Love is not possessive.
　—1 Corinthians 13:4 (NAB)

ONE PERSONALITY TRAIT GETS THE PRIZE FOR RUINING more relationships than any other. It is a characteristic found to some degree in each of us, but when it gets out of hand, it is always destructive and always pushes people away.

I am referring to the tendency to control others. This villain frequently masquerades as love. The overly protective mother will say, "Honey, I'm just doing this for your own good," and the man who constantly corrects his friend thinks, "It's all for his benefit." But the effect is to suffocate, and I have never known a person who did not try to flee from manipulators. Catalog your own aborted friendships—the people you had just as soon not see again. Are they not often those who tried to advise you, dominate you, control you, or judge you?

"At the heart of love," some unknown sage wrote, "there is a simple secret: The lover lets the beloved be free." Those who have successful connections allow their loved ones room. Rather than possessing their friends, they try to help them expand and grow and become free.

So rule number five is:

Create space in your relationships.

In the spring of 1887, a twenty-year-old arrived in Tuscumbia, Alabama, to attempt the tutoring of a deaf-blind girl. The tutor's name was Anne Sullivan and the student's name was Helen Keller. They were to develop one of the most admired friendships of the century.

At seven Helen Keller was a wild vixen who uttered unintelligible animal sounds. When in a rage, she would snatch dishes from the table and throw them and herself on the floor. More than one person had told Mrs. Keller that her child was an idiot.

For weeks Anne spelled words into Helen's small hand, but she could not break through to her consciousness. Then, on April 5, something wonderful happened. Here are Helen Keller's recollections of that day, written more than sixty years later:

> It happened at the well-house, where I was holding a mug under the spout. Annie pumped water into it, and when the water

> gushed out into my hand she kept spelling w-
> a-t-e-r into my other hand with her fingers.
> Suddenly I understood. Caught up in the first
> joy I had known since my illness, I reached out
> eagerly to Annie's ever-ready hand, begging for
> new words to identify whatever objects I
> touched. Spark after spark of meaning flew
> from hand to hand and, miraculously, affec-
> tion was born. From the well-house there
> walked two enraptured beings calling each
> other "Helen" and "Teacher."

Anne Sullivan gave most of her life to Helen
Keller. When her famous pupil decided to go to
college, she sat beside her in every class at Radcliffe,
spelling out the lectures into Helen's hand and
overusing her own defective eyes to spell out books
that were not in Braille.

Anne Sullivan recognized that Helen was a
prodigy and had unlimited possibilities for thinking and feeling. There was no question as to which
of the two had the higher IQ. By the time she was
ten, Helen was writing to famous persons in
Europe *in French*. She quickly mastered five languages and displayed gifts that her teacher never
pretended to have.

But did that change Anne Sullivan's devotion?
Not as far as we know. She was satisfied to be
Helen's companion and encourager, allowing her
to be applauded by kings and presidents and to be
her own unique personage. In short, she gave her
friend room to grow.

The Longing for Freedom

When George and Nena O'Neill interviewed couples for the book *Open Marriage,* they talked to hundreds of people in all types of relationships. Divorced couples. Unmarried couples living together. Couples burned by marriage. Couples successfully married for decades.

Two recurring themes emerged from the data. One was the longing for a committed relationship with someone. The other was a desire for freedom. Although these impulses seem mutually exclusive, the best friendships and the best marriages make room for both. We all require room to breathe. When promising relationships suddenly blow apart, it is often because one partner was manipulated or boxed in.

Unhappily, the tendency to jockey for control and to manipulate our loved ones is being *encouraged* by some of the current pop psychologies. Be more aggressive and more intimidating, so you can become top dog, they tell us. But such a view of interpersonal relationships as battleground is tragic, for it produces loneliness. Winning by intimidation may get sales, but it never gets friends. Any short-term benefits are at the expense of long-term rewards.

If you see all your human contacts as power struggles and if your objective is the domination of others, you might well examine the biography of a man who set such a life goal for himself. He was the central figure in human events between 1933 and 1945, of whom Alan Bullock wrote: "Everything about him was unified around his lust for power and the craving to dominate."

His name was Adolf Hitler.

Albert Speer, who was sucked into Hitler's hypnotic power (and spent twenty years in Spandau prison for his error), reflected later:

> I have never met anyone else in my life with whom I felt this sense of something vital missing. The only times I saw him behave with genuine vivacity and pleasure and spontaneity were when we were together, poring over architectural plans or inspecting his cherished scale models of the Berlin of the future. I don't believe he was capable of real love. Perhaps once in his life he may have been. He had an incestuous affair with his niece, Geli Raubal, whom he drove to suicide.

Are You the Manipulating Type?

Often we control our loved ones without even realizing that we are denying them freedom. Here are three classic types of manipulators who can squeeze the blood out of relationships in a hurry:

The Take-Charge Manipulator: This is the person who must be smarter and stronger than you to be happy with you. Answer the following questions to determine whether you fit:

a. Do we usually end up going to the restaurant or movie I prefer?

b. Do I enjoy correcting factual errors in other people's conversations?

c. Do I use humor to put down my friends?

d. Do I have to know more about a topic than others to feel comfortable discussing it?

If your answers are largely positive, it may be that you are quite insecure. Strange as it may seem, the person who always tries to look superior may have neurotic feelings of inadequacy. The best friendships do not require that anyone keep the upper hand. Rather, there is a mutuality in which either partner is free to be weak at times without fearing that the other will get "one up."

When C. S. Lewis was a young student at Oxford, he made a number of lifelong friends, among them Nevill Coghill and Owen Barfield. Several in that close circle became authors, and they would gather regularly over the years to talk and to read to each other their works in progress. Lewis's reputation soon eclipsed them all, and he turned out increasingly successful books at increasingly shorter intervals. Yet he seemed to appreciate more than ever the old familiar friends. Owen Barfield said: "I never recall a single remark, a single word or silence, a single look . . . which would go to suggest that he felt his opinion was entitled to more respect than that of old friends. . . . I wonder how many famous men there have been of whom this could truthfully be said."

If you are secure, you never have to jockey for control or lord it over your friends, and you know, as Sarah Teasdale once observed, that "no one worth possessing can be quite possessed."

The Poor-Me Manipulator: This person is the direct opposite of the take-charge type, manipulating by appearing weak.

A slightly overweight wife sits in my office with still another set of symptoms, which she calls "anxiety attacks." Her physical problems go through constant mutations. She has been in and out of the hospital, moving from one disaster to another, always in trouble, always an emotional mess.

Yet she is very intelligent, and she seems in some ways to have plenty of ego strength. Why, then, this long parade of calamities? Why is she never able to take charge of her life?

Suddenly it dawns on me. Why didn't I see it sooner? The great tragedy of her childhood had been the day her father left the family for another woman. Her mother was an enterprising type, managed to raise the children well, and eventually remarried. But years later, the next generation's relationships are still governed by that event.

Remembering what happened to her mother, my friend has avoided at all costs the appearance of strength and independence. And, indeed, it seems to work. When she is having an anxiety attack or physical illnesses, her husband hovers over her and is very solicitous. So she puts herself through amazing suffering, convinced that as long as she is in trouble her husband will stay.

Of course, it would be unfair to accuse my friend of deliberately faking sickness in order to hang on to her husband. She is genuinely sick most of the time, and her pain is excruciating. The mechanism is largely unconscious, but it is a powerful form of manipulation just the same.

Such excessive dependency will backfire eventually. Stephanie and Linda have been casual acquaintances since childhood. "We run into each other a couple of times a year," Stephanie says. "Actually, we have a lot of interests in common, and I can tell that Linda is lonely, but she *clutches* at you so. And she talks about her troubles for three hours straight. There's no way I can stand that. I avoid her like the plague."

The Need-to-Be-Needed Manipulator: If you are not the clutching type, do not congratulate yourself too quickly on your independence until you have inquired: Am I on the other end of such friendships and encourage dependence in others?

Here, for instance, is a mother of two married daughters. She does not work outside the home, and she is bored. The housework is done by 10 A.M. One of the few events that relieves her boredom is a call from one of her daughters in trouble—even with a minor problem. Then the engine within suddenly comes alive and adrenaline shoots through her system. She feels needed again! She rushes over to the daughter's house, takes charge, and it's like the old days again.

But it is a dangerous setup, for if she wishes her children to need her that badly, she is likely to foster a sick dependence and keep them as little girls.

How a Famous Couple Combined Closeness and Freedom

Rather than crippling us with dependence, a strong friendship can free us. There are marriages between gifted and aggressive people who nourish each other without worrying about which one has the upper hand.

In the heyday of American magazine publishing, *The Reader's Digest* was printed in thirteen languages, sold thirty million copies a month, and was distributed in 170 countries. The story of how such an empire rose from an initial capitalization of

$1,800 is one of the most stunning success stories in the annals of American publishing. It is also the story of a husband-and-wife partnership.

When DeWitt Wallace was recovering from shrapnel wounds in the army hospital at Aix-les-Bains in 1918, he read every magazine he could lay his hands on. Most of the articles were too long, he thought, and he began experimenting with a way to distill the pieces into a shorter form.

After his discharge DeWitt selected a group of these condensed articles, called the collection *The Reader's Digest,* and sent samples to publishers throughout the country. He proposed to give the *Digest* to any publisher who would retain him as its editor.

The experts were unimpressed. Of the publishers who bothered to reply, only William Randolf Hearst thought the magazine had merit, but he predicted that it would never reach a circulation higher than thirty thousand. It was too small a venture for him to undertake.

DeWitt had gambled everything on the attempt and was bitterly discouraged. He would not realize until later that this rejection of the magazine was a stroke of good fortune.

In Minneapolis, DeWitt found an ally. Lila Bell Acheson, while visiting her brother, met this man with the preposterous idea. She, like DeWitt, was raised in a Presbyterian minister's home and had no money, but before she left Minneapolis, she had fallen in love with DeWitt and was sold on his idea for a periodical.

For the next months, when Lila was in Seattle, DeWitt spent his time mailing circular letters to potential subscribers, each with an individually typed opening page. He had collected a trunk-full of college catalogs, and he sent his appeal for provisional subscriptions to every faculty member listed. He called on women's clubs and professional groups, soliciting subscriptions for the still nonexistent *Reader's Digest*. When he moved to New York he took his trunk with him and continued to send out the furious cloud of appeals.

On October 15, 1921, Lila and DeWitt were married, and before they went off to the Poconos on their wedding trip, he mailed the last circulars.

When the honeymoon couple returned, a bundle of letters awaited them. Remittances now totaled nearly $5,000. They borrowed another $1,300 and placed an order with a Pittsburgh printer for five thousand copies of the first issue. Volume 1, Number 1, appeared in February 1922, with DeWitt Wallace and Lila Bell Acheson as cofounders, coeditors, and co-owners.

But how were they to afford publication of succeeding issues? Rent on their Greenwich Village apartment was paid from Lila's salary as a social worker (she somehow worked eight hours a day and did editorial work at night), and they sublet one room to an NYU instructor and his wife, sharing the bath and kitchen with their tenants. Because they could not afford to subscribe to the magazines from which articles were taken, DeWitt worked at the New York Public Library, laboriously writing in longhand on sheets of yellow paper. He worked until his eyes blurred and his shoulders ached, slipped out to lunch, hurried back.

Soon the magazine's circulation grew beyond the couple's fondest dreams—50,000 in 1926, 228,000 in 1929. The Wallaces found themselves at the head of a publishing phenomenon. One senior editor said of the Wallaces as they neared the end of their long collaboration:

> They have been mutually supportive to the nth degree. He needed a woman who believed in what he was doing, and I'd guess that they talked about manuscripts almost every evening of their married life. Her work was on the art for the magazine, and do you know that when they were in their eighties, she still picked out the covers?

Wallace himself said, "I think Lila made the *Digest* possible."

Friends can be liberating rather then inhibiting, if the two of you can establish from the beginning certain rules for freedom.

Here are six suggestions for creating more space.

1. Be Cautious with Criticism

Some people get a feeling of satisfaction and superiority from criticizing their friends. If you are afflicted with that plague, divest yourself of it as soon as possible. Alice Miller's rule of thumb is a good one: "If it is very painful for you to criticize your friends, you are safe in doing it. But if you take the slightest pleasure in it, that is the time to hold your tongue."

One of the most remarkable things about Jesus was that he was so different from the Pharisees, who devoted themselves to telling people how they should change and shape up. The Pharisees were the self-appointed critics of Christ's day. Possessing what Mark Twain would have labeled a "vinegar piety," they made people nervous. But the common people were drawn to Jesus, in part because his gentleness enabled him to understand the reasons for their mistakes. He recognized that they knew all too well what sinners they were: it wasn't necessary to remind them of that. What they needed was not more feelings of guilt, but salvation.

Ordinary people have always looked askance at the reformer but instinctively loved the saint. The difference is this: reformers focus on the sins of other people, and saints are concerned about their own sins.

D. L. Moody was one of the most powerful Christian evangelists who ever lived. He could hold a crowd in the palm of his hand, won thousands of converts to the faith, and established several religious institutions. Yet he never displayed the pompous air of self-importance that many famous religious leaders did in that era. He was a tolerant, understanding man who rarely criticized. One of his famous sayings was, "Right now I'm having so much trouble with D. L. Moody that I don't have time to find fault with the other fellow."

On the basis of that single quotation, I have always wished that I could have had D. L. Moody for a friend. It would have been relaxing to be around him, for he would have understood that I'm working on my shortcomings. And by that very acceptance, he would have helped me grow. Someone has said, "People have a way of becoming what you encourage them to be—not what you nag them to be," and D. L. Moody was a great encourager.

When all is said and done, a large part of our success at love will depend on our ability to accept human nature as it is. The judgmental temperament never generates much affection. To put it another way, we need to strive for as much understanding of others as we grant ourselves. The Sioux Indians had this rule: "I will not judge my brother until I have walked two weeks in his moccasins." Those who are good at love are always trying to put themselves in the place of their loved ones. In short, they possess tolerance.

Of all the Americans who had this quality, Abraham Lincoln is probably our finest model. With quiet openness he listened to the opinions and feelings of a hoard of critics, office-seekers, and advisors who thought themselves smarter than the president. Through it all he displayed a remarkable benevolence. One of his favorite quotations was, "Judge not, that ye be not judged."

During the Civil War, when Mrs. Lincoln spoke harshly of Southern people, Lincoln replied: "Don't criticize them, Mary; they are just what we would be under similar circumstances."

If we can learn to place ourselves in the shoes of others as Lincoln did, it will be easier to be tolerant.

Beethoven said, "We all make mistakes, but everyone makes different mistakes," and Goethe said, "One has only to grow older to become more tolerant. I see no fault that I might not have committed myself." Samuel Johnson puts the cap on the subject: "God himself, sir, does not propose to judge a man until his life is over. Why should you and I?"

Do not think for a moment that I am urging here that you become a nonassertive blob who agrees with everyone and never expresses an opinion. No, be opinionated. Express your individuality as strongly as you'd like. But be sure to give your friend the same privilege. Assertiveness is okay as long as it is nonpossessive, noninterfering, nondemanding.

2. Employ the Language of Acceptance

We can learn about friendship by looking at how gifted psychologists function, for many clients say that their friendship with some therapist is the best they have ever had with anyone. Dr. Paul Tournier, to whom I referred when discussing transparency, became so famous that many young doctors traveled to Europe to study his techniques. In his typically modest way, Tournier said, "It is a little embarrassing for students to come over to study my 'techniques,' for they always go away disappointed. All I do is accept people."

That was probably the most important single thing that could be said about the art of psychotherapy. If we can learn to acknowledge the integrity of the personality before us, our relationships will be greatly enhanced. That does not mean that we *approve* of everything in the other. Acceptance is an entirely different matter. Much of the material I hear in my office is in conflict with my own moral code: accounts of extramarital affairs, plans that do not seem wise, and crimes of every sort. If I felt compelled to render an opinion about all these matters and to protest when the client is doing something wrong, I'd be putting myself in the place of God. I'd also become barking mad myself.

I've learned that without approving or disapproving of what clients tell me, I can show that I accept them simply by listening. More than anything else, I try to catch the nuances in a person's feelings. It is emotion that we examine most in therapy. A husband talks about how he would like to have an affair with a woman in accounting. A teenager "hates" her alcoholic father and is desperate to leave home. A mother wishes she didn't have children, then feels guilty for having such a terrible thought. These are the raw materials of the therapy session. Through it all I do my best to help people realize that they are entitled to their feelings, that their feelings are neither good nor bad, that it is only when we enter the realm of behavior that we enter the realm of morality, and that talking all this out is healthy.

Dr. Thomas Gordon, in his splendid book *Parent Effectiveness Training,* suggests that in drawing out your children, you employ "door openers" to invite them to talk more and to assure them that you will listen without judging them:

"Really?"

"You did, huh?"

"Interesting."

"Tell me more about it."

"I'd be interested in your point of view."

"This seems like something important to you."

3. Encourage Your Friends to Be Unique

Suggestion number three for loosening up your friendships has to do with the peculiarities of your friends, their eccentricities, their unique dreams. Rather than urging your loved ones to conform, encourage their uniqueness. Everyone has dreams, dreams that no one else has, and you can make yourself loved by encouraging those aspirations.

On May 24, 1965, a strange little craft quietly slipped out of the marina in Falmouth, Massachusetts, and headed its bow to the open ocean. Its lone occupant was Robert Manry, a copy editor for *The Plain Dealer* of Cleveland. After ten years at the copy desk, Manry had decided that he was a crashing bore and had determined that he must do something different. So he had bought a sextant and a navigation book and had begun making plans to pilot his boat, *Tinkerbelle,* to England. At 13 1/2 feet, it would be the smallest craft ever to make the voyage.

Afraid to tell most people his plan for fear they would try to talk him out of it, he simply took a leave of absence from his paper. He did write to a few of his relatives, and his sister wrote back: "It is wonderful to see someone carry out his dream. So few of us take a chance."

But it was his wife, Virginia, who gave him the greatest support. "No one in the world has as wonderful a wife as I," he said later. "Virginia could have insisted that I behave as other rational men did and give up this 'crazy voyage.' But she knew that I was stepping to the music of a different drummer, and she granted me the invaluable boon of self-realization by allowing me to keep pace with the music I heard."

The trip turned out to be anything but a pleasant idyll. He spent harrowing nights of sleeplessness trying to cross shipping lanes without having his midget boat run down by freighters. After weeks at sea the food became tasteless, the loneliness caused him to hallucinate, his rudder broke three times, he was becalmed for days, storms swept him overboard and only the rope around his waist enabled him to climb back on board. But finally, after seventy-eight days at sea, he sailed into Falmouth, England.

During the lonely nights at the tiller, he had often imagined what he would do upon setting foot on land. He had expected to get a hotel room, eat a good dinner in some restaurant alone, and then walk down to the Associated Press office to see if they were interested in his story. But word of his approach had spread. He was quite unprepared for what awaited him. Three hundred vessels escorted him into port, their horns blasting. And forty thousand people, including hordes of reporters, cheered him to shore. He had suddenly become a hero, and his story was told around the world.

But standing on the dock was perhaps the greatest hero of all, his wife, Virginia, who had been flown over by his newspaper. She had the courage to allow her husband the freedom to pursue his dream.

Of course, not every wife is going to allow her mate to risk his life, but it is important to recognize that your loved ones will have unique projects, and if you love them you will love their projects. When do these eccentricities become excessive? Here is a good rule of thumb from William James: "The best position is one of noninterference with another's peculiar ways of being happy, provided that those ways do not interfere by violence with yours."

Like all virtues carried too far, it is possible for freedom to become a vice. The philosophy, "You do your thing, and I'll do mine," if allowed to become the keystone of a relationship, means that you no longer have a relationship. Commitment is also essential. Different people require different amounts of independence, and the mix may need to be renegotiated from time to time.

4. Allow for Solitude

A nonpossessive friendship will maintain a profound respect for each person's need for privacy. There is such a thing as too much closeness. In all our relationships we move together and apart at various times, like a dance. It is one of the marks of a mature relationship that you can relax if your friend is moving away from you for a while.

Dr. Lawrence Hattere, associate clinical professor of psychiatry at Cornell Medical School, says, "I have several artist friends who are busy and creative and very private people. I see them infrequently. Yet with them I'm more intimate and can often speak more openly than with some of the people I see every day."

Children, in particular, require privacy to dream, to rehearse, to explore their own wild and wonderful imaginations. Some parents know this. Five-year-old Bill was upstairs one day when a friend stopped by to see his mother. An hour passed, and to the visitor, Bill's silence was ominous. "What's he doing up there?" she asked.

His mother smiled serenely. "Who knows? Sometimes when he's quiet, he's a Native American stalking a bear, or a spaceman listening. He creates his own universe, and I never enter it unless I'm invited."

She understands that in affording privacy to children we are assuring them that their faith in themselves is justified.

The same applies to marriage. It is possible to be together so much that we suffocate each other. Here is Rainer Maria Rilke's comment:

> A good marriage is that in which [one] . . . appoints the other guardian of [one's] . . . solitude. Once the realization is accepted that even between the closest human beings infinite distances continue to exist, a wonderful living side by side can grow up, if they succeed in loving the distance between them which makes it possible for each to see the other whole against a wide sky!

5. Encourage Other Relationships

Jealousy, according to one of Shakespeare's characters, is a "green-eyed monster," and it has ruined many intimate friendships. If you get nervous when your best friend spends time with other friends or when a couple you and your mate enjoy excludes you from some of their social activities, you need to be wary of the corroding effect of jealousy. You never have exclusive rights to anyone, and you hobble people if you expect to be the only person who matters to them.

Clutching behavior comes from overworking and overloading one relationship. The antidote for jealousy is to expand your own interests and to make friends in several groupings. Your life must encompass multiple interests, passions in many areas, and several relationships if you are to avoid crowding any of your loved ones.

For instance, some people miss a lot of the love available to them because they somewhere heard the canard that happily married people should not require friends. When a client says, "My husband is the only friend I need, we tell each other everything," it makes me nervous. That puts a tremendous amount of pressure on the marriage. As wonderful as marriage can be, no one person can meet all your needs, and you do well to explore another whole realm of nonsexual relationships. Your mate ought to be your best friend, but not your only one.

Two people enter another trap if they suppose that after marriage they should give up their old friends from single days and find new couples with whom they can spend evenings. The odds of four people all liking each other equally are almost impossible. When a husband and wife do find another couple with whom they are *simpatico,* they are fortunate. But when it does not happen—and it is not likely to happen often—one should not hesitate to develop strong personal connections in which one's mate may not want to participate.

Marge and Julie were in the same sorority in college and were in each other's weddings. At first, when each had small children at home, they did not talk often and seemed to drift apart. But now they live nearer and they frequently have a long lunch in some restaurant. Their husbands do not have much in common, and efforts to get together as a foursome did not work.

"When Marge and I finally woke up to the fact that our husbands would rather have us get together on our own," says Julie, "and we stopped feeling guilty about having lunch as often as we felt like it, it really freed up our friendship. We're both nuts about Bach, which Alan and Mark can't stand, so sometimes we even leave them home with the kids at night and go to an organ concert together. When I come home to Alan those nights, I cuddle up to him in bed and I'm really grateful that he doesn't expect us to share everything. Funny thing, though. I feel good to have something new to tell him. That's half the fun of those concerts—coming home and telling Alan about what the music did to me." Marge's and Julie's marriages are enriched, not diminished, by their relationship.

6. Be Ready for Shifts in Your Friendships

Let us say your little sister tagged along with you as you were growing up and you were clearly the dominant one. If you are to have a healthy connection as adults, you must give her more room, allow her to be an adult, make her your equal. That is difficult, for years of conditioning have created a lopsided alliance. But it must change, and it can if you are prepared for shifting relationships.

The same modulation is necessary in freeing our teenage children. It seems only a short time ago that we were tying their shoelaces and taking their hand as they crossed the street. At a certain age we must quickly unlearn our relational habits and remind ourselves again and again that they are no longer little children who are dependent on us.

As a smart mother quoted to me once, "There are two lasting things you should give your children: One of these is roots; the other is wings." She paused a minute, then added, "The first is easier than the second."

Father Henri Nouwen used the metaphor of hospitality in urging that we grant freedom to our children:

> It may sound strange to speak of the relationship between parents and children in terms of hospitality. But it belongs to the center of the Christian message that children are not properties to own and rule over, but gifts to cherish and care for. Our children are our most important guests, who enter into our home, ask for careful attention, stay for a while and then leave to follow their own way.

I wish all of the parents who enter my office for help with a child's emotional problems would post that quotation on the bathroom mirror and read it five times a day. For I see again and again the carnage left behind when a parent substituted manipulation for love.

If you want to read a splendid book about parenting in general and about how much freedom to give your teenager in particular, I recommend a very readable little volume by my friend Charlie Shedd titled *Promises to Peter*. (It is out of print, but used copies are available at used bookstores and often at on-line bookstores.) When our children were at home my wife and I tried to read it once a year. Dr. Shedd describes in detail his and Martha's plan of "growing self-government" for their children. You may not want to give your youngster as much latitude as they did in the Shedd house, but *some* such plan for gradual emancipation must go into effect or you'll lose your children as friends.

Anthropologist Gregory Bateson was the first to distinguish between complementary and symmetrical types of relationships. According to Bateson, behavior between unequal parties is "complementary," involving dependency and nurturance, superiority and inferiority. "Symmetrical" was his term for the relationships between peers. To use his language, our relationships with our children must shift from complementary to symmetrical.

Keep in mind, however, that such a shift is as difficult for your child as it is for you. To understand your child's confusion, you need only think about how you relate to your parents. Even when you have children and grandchildren of your own, you may find yourself acting like a child again when you are in your parents' presence.

A great Scandinavian actress with worldwide fame and with a daughter of her own was asked if she could relate to her mother as one adult to another. "I would love to," she said. "It's my big dream. But my mother insists to be the mother and I am the daughter. She does it without knowing it, because she claims she doesn't do it; and that's the way it will be forever, you know. Maybe it's my fault too because also without knowing it, I think, I cater to being the daughter. But I really would love to have her as a friend. I would love to know who she really is. What are her thoughts, her disappointments, her hopes, as a woman—not as a mother I know, but a woman."

These are not easy shoals to negotiate, but the people around us are constantly changing, so healthy relationships must maintain an elasticity in order to accommodate to these shifts.

Rule number five, then, for deepening your friendships is:

Create space in your relationships.

PART II

FIVE GUIDELINES

FOR CULTIVATING INTIMACY

CHAPTER 7

Please Touch

*There is one temple in the universe—the human body.
We touch heaven when we touch the human body.*
　—Thomas Carlyle

A FEW YEARS AGO A GROUP OF YOUNG MEDICAL
students was training in the children's ward of a
large eastern hospital. One student seemed especially loved by the children. They always greeted
him with joy.

The others could not understand why. Finally
they detailed one of their number to follow him
and find out what he did. The observer detected
nothing until night, when the young medic made
his last round. Then the mystery was solved. He
kissed every child good-night.

Guideline number one for cultivating intimacy is:

Use your body to demonstrate warmth.

The Most Powerful Organ of the Body

Our bodies can become our best tools for achieving genuine intimacy with those around us. If you observe those who have deep relationships, you will find that, although few of them are indiscriminate grabbers who hug everyone in sight, most have delicately tuned their sense of touch and it is in use every time they are with people. They listen with their eyes, they draw close to another person during conversation, and they make body contact frequently to keep the communication at a warm level.

Ashley Montagu wrote a long and scholarly book on the art of touching. He demonstrated that the skin, once regarded as little more than a simple body covering, is actually our most powerful sense organ. More than half a million sensory fibers flow from the skin through the spinal cord to the brain. As a sensory system it is quite remarkable. A human being can function blind and deaf and completely lacking the senses of smell or taste, but it is impossible to survive at all without the function performed by the skin. It was once thought that animals licked their young merely to keep them clean. But as Montagu has shown, the washing serves a much more profound purpose. Proper stimulation of the skin is essential for organic and behavioral development.

The Universal Longing to Be Touched

The young of all mammals snuggle and cuddle against the body of the mother and against the bodies of their siblings. Almost every animal enjoys being stroked or otherwise having its skin pleasurably stimulated. Dogs appear to be insatiable in their appetite for petting, cats will purr for it, and dolphins love to be gently stroked.

For a period during the 19th century more than half of the infants died in their first year of life, many from a disease called *marasmus,* a Greek word meaning "wasting away." As late as the 1920s, according to Montagu, the death rate for infants under one year of age in various U.S. foundling institutions was close to 100 percent. Dr. Henry Chapin's detective work on this alarming phenomenon is a fascinating tale.

A distinguished New York pediatrician, Chapin noted that the infants were kept in sterile, neat, tidy wards, but were rarely picked up. Chapin brought in women to hold the babies, coo to them, and stroke them, and the mortality rate dropped drastically.

Who was responsible for all those babies who had died unnecessarily? Not the foundling home directors, for they were operating on the best "scientific" information available to them. The real villain was one Emmett Holt Sr., professor of pediatrics at Columbia University. Holt was the author of the booklet *The Care and Feeding of Children,* which was first published in 1894 and was in its 15th edition in 1935. During its long ascendancy, it was the supreme authority, the Dr. Spock of its time. And it was in this book that the author urged mothers to abolish the cradle and refuse to pick up the baby when it cried, for fear of spoiling it with too much handling. Tender loving care would have been considered "unscientific."

We now know that small children become irritable and hyperactive without adequate body contact.

In various experiments with normal and subnormal youngsters, those who had the most physical contact with parents or attendants learned to walk and talk the earliest and had the highest IQs.

The young desperately crave physical affection. Howard Maxwell of Los Angeles is a man in tune with his time. So when his four-year-old daughter Melinda acquired a fixation for "The Three Little Pigs" and demanded that he read it to her night after night, Mr. Maxwell, very pleased with himself, tape-recorded the story. When Melinda next asked for it, he simply switched on the machine. This worked for a couple of nights, but then one evening Melinda pushed the storybook at her father.

"Now, honey," he said, "you know how to turn on the recorder."

"Yes," said Melinda, "but I can't sit on its lap."

Many parents stop touching their children at about the age of five or six, and soon after that the children stop touching one another. They bow slowly to the immense social pressure in our culture, which regards tactile deprivation as normal for adults. But in Asia, for instance, it is common to see two heterosexual friends of the same sex walking with each other hand in hand. Whereas Italians and French touch each other up to a hundred times an hour during conversation, Americans, on average, make contact fewer than three times.

Gordon Inkeles, who has taught massage at universities throughout the United States, says that the skin of most adult Americans is starved. "That the skin has been starved for the better part of a lifetime is never more apparent than in the afterglow of a two-hour body massage," he writes. "In those silent moments one often discovers on the most ordinary faces the kind of expressions usually reserved for saints and swamis."

There are only two situations in which most of us will allow another adult to touch us: during sex, and during treatments by individuals who are licensed to touch—tailors, hairdressers, masseurs, physical therapists. These professionals are usually careful to remain as cold as possible, lest their touching be construed as a sexual advance. But beyond the intimacies of sex and professional body contact is a whole range of tactile experiences and personal communication.

Following Jesus in his contacts with the peasant people of Palestine, one sees him touching again and again. He "stretched out his hand and touched" the leper, for instance (Matt. 8:3). When Peter's mother-in-law was sick, Jesus "touched her hand, and the fever left her" (Matt. 8:15), and when mothers brought their little children to him, "he took them up in his arms, laid his hands on them, and blessed them (Mark 10:16).

How to Communicate Warmth Without Saying a Word

Actress Melina Mercouri's autobiography, *I Was Born Greek,* starts:

> The first man I loved was Spiros. He was extremely handsome, extremely seductive. His mouth smelled sweeter than any man's I've ever known. I adored his embrace, an embrace scented of rosewater and basil. He was strong.

He was tall. He had a passion for me. It made
my childhood a very happy one. Spiros was my
grandfather.

If you want to get closer to those around you, be
aware of the power of communication that you
hold in your hands. In my work I am sometimes at
a loss to know what to say in the face of the complex problems presented by clients. Sometimes I
impulsively reach out and put my hand on their
arms or hands in an attempt to convey how keenly
I respond to what they are telling me.

One day a waif of a teenager came to her
appointment distraught and upset. During most of
the session she wept uncontrollably. The following
week I was prepared to resume our discussion of
the topic, but to my amazement she could not
recall what our topic had been! What she remem-
bered about the session was that I had hugged her
on her way out. Both men and women confide
often that the thing they long for most is to be able
to go to their mate and be held for a while.

Physical gushing is as offensive as verbal gushing, but when it is a genuine expression of your
affection, touch can bring you closer to another
than thousands of words. Men can find masculine
ways of giving an affectionate message to other
men. Get into the habit of shaking hands. The act
of your going to the person and getting the close
proximity of your bodies necessary for the handshake conveys a message. A pat on the back, a play-
ful punch in the stomach, or your hand on a man's
shoulder as you talk—all these should be in your
vocabulary of gestures.

In our contacts with the opposite sex, touching need not always have a sexual connotation. We can give encouragement, offer comfort, or express tenderness with physical demonstrations.

When Mark's alcoholism had its tightest grip on him, Mondays were the worst. After a weekend of steady drinking, he would somehow drag himself to work on Monday morning, but the day was eight hours of torture. "When I'd come home," he said, "I'd glance at the mail and head for the bedroom with the paper. I wouldn't want to talk to anybody. But many times, as I lay there on top of the bed, my daughter Katrina would come in to say hello. She'd see that I was feeling terrible and somehow knew how badly I needed support, although I couldn't ask for it. So she'd lie down beside me, touching my arm while I read the paper. Without words between us, I could feel the poisons being drained off by her presence."

It is not accidental that the Bible prescribes the laying on of hands as part of Christian healing. We can often do more than we realize with touch.

The Sensual Touch

Intimacy with your mate is of course enormously enhanced by sensual stimulation and by sex itself. In the passion of making love, many of us are able to communicate a profundity of love that words cannot carry. But it is a mistake to limit our physical contact to basic sexual intercourse. We supposedly live in an era of sexual expression and the breakdown of taboos, yet couples still tend to ignore most of their partners' bodies. Sexually free lovers know all about the so-called erogenous zones, but many ignore the remaining 95 percent of the body.

In our work with couples who have some sexual dysfunction—most commonly now a decrease in libido in one or both of the partners—my colleagues and I almost always find that the husband and wife are literally "out of touch" with each other. That is, the caressing, fondling, embracing, and kissing that once were central to the bond between them have gradually diminished. It is no wonder, then, that they have developed sexual problems.

The treatment is basically the same for all such problems: We get them back to touching each other. We often suggest that they look at some of the many books and tapes now available on the ancient art of Tantra. Some misunderstanding persists about this approach to sex. It is not avoiding orgasm. It is simply prolonging the experiences prior to and following orgasm. You slowly explore each other's bodies, looking for the places your mate especially enjoys tonight. Then once coitus begins, you extend that also. Too many of us, once we start intercourse, work as hard as possible to bring our mate and ourselves to an orgasm as quickly as possible. Tantra teaches one to prolong the experience, to hold back from orgasms for a long period, staying at a high level of sexual arousal. It is something like a surfer riding the crest of a wave.

Many couples come back to our office after learning these techniques at home and report that they received as much joy from caressing as from being caressed. Some people, married twenty or thirty years, will say, "You know, I never fully explored my mate's body before, and it's terrific!" Without asking, I know the mate liked it, too.

We find that if a husband and wife who differ in how often they would like to make love will spend leisurely amounts of time caressing each other, their sexual needs will level out somewhat. The partner who formerly complained about not getting enough sex (usually the husband) is content with less frequent intercourse because of the glow he gets from intense touching, and the partner who formerly was turned off much of the time becomes highly aroused by these new experiences and desires more frequent lovemaking.

Guideline number one, then, for cultivating intimacy with your loved ones:

Use your body to demonstrate warmth.

CHAPTER 8

The Art of Affirmation

I can live for two months on one good compliment.
　—Mark Twain

SOME FASCINATING PSYCHOLOGICAL DETECTIVE WORK was once done in a second-grade classroom. The teacher had complained that the children were getting harder and harder to control. They were standing up and roaming around the room rather than doing their work.

Two psychologists spent many days at the back of the room with stopwatches, carefully observing the behavior of both the children and the teacher. Every ten seconds they recorded on their pads how many children were out of their seats. On the average, some child was standing 360 times in every twenty-minute period and the teacher said "Sit down!" seven times in every twenty-minute period.

The psychologists suggested that she consciously increase the number of times she commanded, "Sit down!" and see what would happen. So in the next few days, according to the observers, she yelled, "Sit down!" an average of 27.5 times per twenty-minute period. Did that change the children's behavior? Indeed it did. They were out of their seats 540 times per period, or *an increase of about 50 percent.* To check their data, the researchers asked the teacher to return to her normal number of reprimands and the level of roaming declined to almost exactly the normal rate within two days. Then for another two days the "Sit down!" commands were increased, and sure enough, the number of children out of their seats increased again.

Here is the kicker. For the final week, the psychologists asked that the teacher refrain entirely from yelling, "Sit down!" and instead quietly compliment children who were staying in their seats doing their work. The result? *The roaming around decreased by 33 percent, the best behavior for the entire experiment.*

The lesson is obvious: Children will increase whatever behavior gets them attention, even if it is negative attention. Parents who harshly discipline their children when they fight and ignore them when they are playing nicely, supposing that they do not require attention then, are headed for disaster.

But these principles were not discovered as recently as the advent of behavior modification. Lincoln often repeated the saying, "A drop of honey catches more flies than a gallon of gall."

So if you are looking for a way to increase your success with people, master the art of affirmation. What worked in the Wisconsin classroom will work with your employees, your clients, your teachers, and your mate. There is magic in the compliment.

Guideline number two for cultivating intimacy is simply:

Be liberal with praise.

In 1936 a book was published by an unknown YMCA instructor. He had resigned a good-paying sales job and left Warrensburg, Missouri, with the hope of teaching some of the principles of public speaking and human relations he had learned as a salesman. The directors of the twenty-third street YMCA in New York City couldn't afford to pay him the regular $2 teaching fee for a course that was untried and unknown. But when he persisted and offered to organize and teach the course on a commission basis, the directors agreed to let him give it a try.

Within two years the course was so popular that the young man was earning thirty dollars a night instead of two. A publishing executive enrolled in the course in Larchmont, New York. He was sufficiently impressed with the material on human relations that he encouraged the instructor to gather it into a book. The young man's name was Dale Carnegie, and when his book, *How to Win Friends and Influence People,* was published, it stayed on *The New York Times* best-seller list for ten years. After selling more than thirteen million copies, the book continues to sell at the rate of more than one hundred thousand every year.

What is the distilled wisdom of Mr. Carnegie's book? It is contained in his chapter, "The Big Secret of Dealing with People," and it is the theme of fully five sections of the book. Not that the idea is original with Mr. Carnegie. Every successful lover, every first-rate manager, every good parent employs this technique every day. You have used it when you've been at your best with others. Carnegie encapsulates it this way: "Be hearty in your approbation and lavish in your praise."

Mr. Charles Schwab was one of the first men ever to earn a million dollars a year. Why did Andrew Carnegie pay Schwab more than $3,000 a day to run his steel company? Because he knew more about the manufacture of steel than other people? No. Schwab said that he had many men working for him whose technical knowledge surpassed his.

Schwab was paid such a handsome amount largely because of his ability to deal with people. Here is the secret set down in his own words:

> I consider my ability to arouse enthusiasm among the men the greatest asset I possess, and the way to develop the best that is in a man is by appreciation and encouragement. There is nothing else that so kills the ambitions of man as criticisms from his superiors. . . . I believe in giving a man incentive to work. So I am anxious to praise but loath to find fault. If I like anything, I am hearty in my approbation and lavish in my praise.

So-called intellectuals have had lots of fun attacking such techniques as dishonest and manipulative. *How to Win Friends and Influence People* has been parodied a dozen times as naïve psychology. But what's simpleminded or manipulative about telling people something you like about them? Affirmation merely for the sake of making another person happy can be a most pleasant activity. Let me illustrate with an incident from Dale Carnegie's own history:

> I was waiting in line to register a letter in the post office at Thirty-third Street and Eighth Avenue in New York. I noticed that the registry clerk was bored with his job—weighing envelopes, handing out stamps, making change, issuing receipts—the same monotonous grind year after year. So I said to myself: "I am going to try to make that chap like me. Obviously, to make him like me, I must say something nice, not about myself, but about him." So I asked myself, "What is there about him that I can honestly admire?" That is sometimes a hard question to answer, especially with strangers; but in this case, it happened to be easy. I instantly saw something I admired no end.
>
> So while he was weighing my envelope, I remarked with enthusiasm: "I certainly wish I had your head of hair."
>
> He looked up, half-startled, his face beaming with smiles. "Well, it isn't as good as it used to be," he said modestly. I assured him that although it might have lost some of its pristine glory, nevertheless it was still magnificent. He was immensely pleased. We carried

on a pleasant conversation and the last thing he said to me was: "Many people have admired my hair."

I told this story once in public; and a man asked me afterwards: "What did you want to get out of him?"

What was I trying to get out of him!!! What was I trying to get out of him!!!

If we are so contemptibly selfish that we can't radiate a little happiness and pass on a bit of honest appreciation without trying to screw something out of the other person in return . . . we shall meet with the failure we so richly deserve.

Oh, yes, I did want something out of that chap. I wanted something priceless. And I got it. I got the feeling that I had done something for him without his being able to do anything whatever in return for me. That is a feeling that glows and sings in your memory long after the incident has passed.

If you train your mind to search for the positive aspects in other people, you will be surprised at how many good things you can observe in them and comment upon. Ralph Waldo Emerson said, "Every man I meet is my superior in some way." If an American giant like Emerson could say that, it should not be too hard for us ordinary people to discover the outstanding qualities of our neighbors.

The art of affirmation is enhanced if we learn to express praise when it is not expected. There are certain occasions, such as after a well-prepared meal or a fine speech, when it is mere social custom to compliment. Sir Henry Taylor, in his 19th-century book *The Statesman,* makes the point that to wait and recall the details of an incident later will be more effective.

> Applaud a man's speech at the moment when he sits down and he will take your compliment as exacted by the demands of common civility; but let some space intervene, and then show him that the merits of his speech have dwelt with you when you might have been expected to have forgotten them, and he will remember your compliment for a much longer time than you have remembered his speech.

Instilling Self-Confidence

If you develop the golden habit of expressing appreciation for the persons with whom you associate, you'll see a cumulative effect. Dr. Paul Roberts, the child psychologist, once said that regular messages of acceptance and love are highly important in establishing a child's self-image. According to Roberts, the accumulation of such messages leads a child to conclude, "I know they accept me," not "Maybe they do and maybe they don't—I'll see how they react next time." When positive information has built up, the child can ride through a scolding from adults or rejection from other children.

Can parents really do much to encourage self-reliance? "Yes they can," says Ruth Stafford Peale.

The secret is this: watch to see where a child's innate skills or talents lie, then gently (do not expect too much too soon) lead or coax him or her in those areas. It may be difficult for a father who was a crack athlete to understand and help a son who would rather play chess than football. But chess, not football, is what such a boy needs if confidence is to grow in him. If he does that one thing well he will come to believe that he can do other things well, and he won't be afraid to attempt them.

In choosing to give or withhold affirmation, we have considerable control over the other person's self-image. In one of our therapy groups we were discussing body image, and different people were telling how they saw themselves. A tall, slender young woman with beautiful long hair said:

"I see myself as fat and pimply."

"You mean you used to be fat with pimples?" someone asked.

"No, that's how I think of myself now."

The group couldn't believe what they were hearing. If anything, the lady was *skinny,* and she had fine, clear skin. Why then the distorted self-perception? No doubt at some stage of her growth, probably in early adolescence, she had been unattractive, perhaps with acne. Perhaps someone had made fun of her body. That picture was etched in her mind, and no one had bothered to change it. Here was a gorgeous woman who did not know she was beautiful because she had an inner filter that kept her from hearing any compliments—if and when they were given. Understanding this, the

group became very assertive, ferreted out that filter, and she blossomed before our eyes.

The Power to Draw Out the Best

"Applause is a spur to noble minds," someone said,
and we all have access to enormous power—the
ability to spur others on by our praise.
Affirmations cost nothing, yet people around us
would do anything to be praised for something.
The pioneering American psychologist William
James said: "The deepest principle in human
nature is the craving to be appreciated." Note his
choice of words. He did not speak of the "hope" or
"desire." He said "craving."

Dale Carnegie says of the desire for praise: "The
rare individual[s] who honestly satisf[y] this heart-
hunger will hold people in the palm of [their]
hand and even the undertaker will be sorry when
[they] die."

Gandhi inspired millions of people to go
beyond their native limits and to accomplish
unheard-of feats. Louis Fischer, one of Gandhi's
most important biographers, gives a clue to the
Indian leader's genius for inspiring people: "He
refused to see the bad in people. He often changed
human beings by regarding them not as what they
were but as though they were what they wished to
be, and as though the good in them was all of
them."

Most of us have been fortunate enough to have
someone early in our lives—a teacher, a grandpar-
ent, a friend—who took a particular interest in us,
passing over our foolish weak aspects and drawing
into the light those strong aspects that no one else

had looked quite far enough to find. If you will affirm others around you in that way, you will put them forever in your debt, and you will linger in their minds long after you are gone.

When Anne Morrow met Charles Lindbergh, he was a national hero. He had won about $500,000 (in today's dollars) for crossing the Atlantic, and was flying from city to city, promoting aviation. Anne's father was ambassador to Mexico. During Lindbergh's visit to Mexico for the State Department, a love began to grow between the two young people. It was to bind them together for forty-seven years. Anne was, like her husband, shy and retiring, but despite tragedies in their life and despite being married to a man always in the limelight, she went on to become one of America's most popular authors.

Describing their marriage, she gives a clue to the success of her career. Her husband believed in her to an extraordinary degree. She says:

> To be deeply in love is, of course, a great liberating force and the most common experience that frees. . . . Ideally, both members of a couple in love free each other to new and different worlds. I was no exception to the general rule. The sheer fact of finding myself loved was unbelievable and changed my world, my feelings about life and myself. I was given confidence, strength, and almost a new character. The man I was to marry believed in me and what I could do, and consequently I found I could do more than I realized.

Here is a story my friend Bruce Larson tells in his own words:

Early one morning I had to catch a plane from Newark, New Jersey, to Syracuse, New York, having returned late the previous night from leading one conference and on my way to another.

I was tired. I had not budgeted my time wisely and I was totally unprepared for the intense schedule before me. After rising early and hastily eating breakfast, I drove to the airport in a mood that was anything but positive. By the time the plane took off I felt so sorry for myself.

Sitting on the plane with an open notebook in my lap, I prayed, "O God, help me. Let me get something down here that will be useful to your people in Syracuse."

Nothing came. I jotted down phrases at random, feeling worse by the moment, and more and more guilty. Such a situation is a form of . . . insanity. It denies all that we know about God himself and his ability to redeem any situation.

About halfway through the brief flight, a stewardess came down the aisle passing out coffee. All the passengers were men, as women have too much sense to fly at seven o'clock in the morning. As the stewardess approached my seat, I heard her exclaim, "Hey! Someone is wearing English Leather aftershave lotion. I can't resist a man who wears English Leather. Who is it?"

Eagerly I waved my hand and announced, "It's me."

The stewardess immediately came over and sniffed my cheek, while I sat basking in this sudden attention and appreciating the covetous glances from passengers nearby.

All through the remainder of the flight the stewardess and I maintained a cheerful banter each time she passed my seat. She would make some comment and I would respond gaily. Twenty-five minutes later when the plane prepared to land I realized that my [low spirits] . . . had vanished. Despite the fact that I had failed in every way—in budgeting my time, in preparation, in attitude—everything had changed. I was freshly aware that I loved God and that he loved me in spite of my failure.

What is more, I loved myself and the people around me and the people who were waiting for me in Syracuse. I was like the Gadarene demoniac after Jesus had touched him: clothed, in my right mind, and seated at the feet of Jesus. I looked down at the notebook in my lap and found a page full of ideas that could prove useful throughout the weekend.

"God," I mused, "how did this happen?" It was then that I realized that someone had entered my life and turned a key. It was just a small key, turned by a very unlikely person. But that simple act of affirmation, that undeserved and unexpected attention, had got me back into the stream.

The art of affirmation is an almost miraculous key. Pablo Casals said, "As long as one can admire and love, then one is young forever." So guideline number two for cultivating intimacy is:

Be liberal with praise.

CHAPTER 9

A Coffee-Cup Concept of Marriage

We discovered a terrific four-letter word for psychotherapy: talk.
   —Penni and Richard Crenna

Dear Ann Landers:

My husband doesn't talk to me. He just sits there night after night, reading the newspaper or looking at TV. When I ask him a question, he grunts 'hu, 'unhu, or uh'huh. Sometimes he doesn't even grunt. All he really needs is a housekeeper and somebody to sleep with him when he feels like it. He can buy both. There are times when I wonder why he got married.

SUCH COMPLAINTS ARE NOT UNCOMMON. FOR reasons that are not altogether clear, many of us have a tendency to stop talking to those we love the longer we have known them.

Some time ago a psychologist ran an experiment measuring the amount of conversation that occurs between the average wife and husband in a week's time. To make the experiment accurate, the researcher strapped portable electronic microphones to the subjects and measured every word they uttered—idle conversation while driving to the store, requests to pass the toast, everything.

There are 168 hours in a week, 10,080 minutes. How much of that time do you suppose the average couple devoted to talking to each other? No, not ten hours, not a single hour, nor even thirty minutes. The conversation took, on the average, a grand total of seventeen minutes. "Loneliness," says Germaine Greer, "is never more cruel than when it is felt in close propinquity with someone who has ceased to communicate."

Why One Woman Had an Affair

Talk is cheap, they say, but it is an essential ingredient in the best relationships. A woman sat in my office who had been married many years and had recently begun an affair with another man. I assumed that most of the energy in their clandestine meetings was sexual. "No," she said. "To tell you the truth, I've only slept with him two or three times, and it wasn't all that great then. The reason I'm so in love with him and want to be with him anytime I can is that we can *talk*. We discuss things for hours on end. Gosh! It's great to talk to a man like that—to tell him everything that's in your heart, and have him do the same with you. Why don't my husband and I ever communicate like that?"

There are probably a lot of reasons she and her husband don't communicate like that, one of which may be that her husband does not recognize how important talk is.

Eric Hoffer was a San Francisco dockworker who spent his evenings writing books about philosophy. *The True Believer, The Ordeal of Change,* and *The Passionate State of Mind* eventually made him famous. Hoffer's childhood was very difficult. His mother died when he was seven, and later the same year Hoffer suddenly and inexplicably went blind. Until his eyesight was restored when he was fifteen, a Bavarian peasant woman cared for him. She taught Hoffer the importance of talk. He writes of her:

> This woman must have really loved me, because those eight years of blindness are in my mind as a happy time. I remember a lot of talk and laughter. I must have talked a great deal, because Martha used to say again and again, "I remember you said this, you remember you said that." . . . She remembered everything I said, and all my life I have had the feeling that what I think and what I say are worth remembering. She gave me that.

Of course, chatter does not necessarily lead to closeness. There are many kinds of talk, and the mere flow of words between two people does not guarantee intimacy. Nevertheless, there can be no intimacy *without* conversation. To know and love a friend over the years, you must have regular talks. This may seem obvious, but I see many close relationships break down because the talk dried up. Guideline number three, then, for cultivating intimacy is:

Schedule leisurely breaks for conversation.

Stan and Richard have played golf every Thursday afternoon for more than ten years. They are very different types of men. Stan owns a small electronic repair business, and Richard is a commercial artist. But their afternoon on the links is an important ritual that neither violates if he is in town.

"We say we do it for the exercise and the chance to be outdoors," says Stan, "but the real reason we get together—and we both know it—is to talk. We need to log in with each other at least once a week."

Last year Richard lost his job and was out of work for almost six months. He says that the Thursday afternoon talks were one of the things that pulled him through.

A Plan for Talk

Charlie Shedd wrote more wisely and wittily on the subject of marriage than anyone else. He had a right to talk. He raised five children, and he and Martha had one of the best marriages in America. In one of his books, he discloses two appointments with his wife that helped keep their vibrations sweet: once a week out together for dinner alone, and fifteen minutes a day visiting in depth.

The first is a dinner date for each other only. No guests. No entertaining. "Sometimes it's a lunch," he explains, "but wherever and whenever, we put our elbows on the table for a deep look. Far down into each other's souls we look."

The second appointment—fifteen minutes a day visiting in depth—is not for discussion of bills or children's problems or planning the weekend picnic. The subject is, "What's going on inside Martha and Charlie?"

Another couple I know reports that theirs is a "coffee-cup concept of marriage." They mean that when dinner is over and the dishes are in the dishwasher, the two of them pour another cup of coffee and sit down at the table to tell each other about the day. Part of the attraction of that cup of coffee is revealed by the husband: "I guess if I ever understood my wife completely our life would be much less interesting. But she's never lost a certain mystery for me, and I always look forward to the evening visits because I know I'm going to find out something new."

Still another couple finds that they need to walk down to a nearby cafe to talk about serious things. In your house it is easy to let your hands get distracted with folding clothes or to let your eyes wander over to the TV when your partner is talking. You might try asking your spouse out for coffee, facing each other with your hands touching, and see what a difference your undivided attention makes.

The point is that good, rich conversation is possible if we seek it.

How to Talk with Kids

Time for talk is equally important with your children. Charlie Shedd had another secret that might work at your house. When his children were growing up, he took each child out for dinner alone monthly. The kids got to choose the restaurant. And after they'd had a good talk, they went to a store and bought something for the child. Shedd said that even when his children reached what he calls the "cave years" (the adolescent period when they don't talk to the family, live in the clutter they call a room, and come out three times a day to eat and grunt at the family), they still enjoyed those regular talks. "Sometimes, just for effect," he reported, "I have said to one of the cave dwellers, 'This is our Saturday out! You rather not go?' Would you believe? Never a single turndown."

Talking Requires Effort

One reason we avoid regular periods of sustained conversation with our intimates is that it sometimes requires a great deal of energy. A single mother relates her effort to spend half an hour of quiet time with her young children before she puts them to bed. "We spend that time planning things we're going to do, or discussing what has happened that day, or just hanging out, which is the hardest for a type A person. I'm pretty good at doing things with my kids—telling stories, playing games, fixing their meals—but sitting down and talking is tough."

It may be tough all right, but those kids are lucky to have a mother who works at it. If we get so busy with our sewing projects or corporate meetings that we do not have time to visit with our children, we are too busy.

One day when Francis Xavier, weary from his arduous missionary labors, went to his room to rest, he gave strict orders that under no circumstances was he to be disturbed. But before long his door opened, and he reappeared long enough to say, "If it is a child that comes, awaken me."

Guideline number three for cultivating intimacy is:

Schedule leisurely breaks for conversation.

CHAPTER 10

How to Improve Your Conversational Skills

The first duty of love is to listen.
  —Paul Tillich

I ONCE KNEW A WOMAN WHO HATED PARTIES. "Before going to a social engagement," she said, "I'd tell myself: 'Now try hard. Be lively. Say bright things. Talk.' But to keep up that front, I'd end up drinking a lot and I'd come home depressed. I just didn't seem to fit.

"But now before going to a party," she says, "I just tell myself to listen with affection to anyone who talks to me, to be in their shoes when they talk, to try to know them without my mind pressing against theirs, or arguing, or changing the subject. My attitude is: Tell me more. This person is showing me his soul. It is a little dry and meager and full of small talk just now, but presently he will

113

begin to show his true self. Then he will be wonderfully alive."

It doesn't take a psychologist to know that, with her new attitude, she is now sought after by plenty of people. She has learned the art of drawing out the other person in conversation. Guideline number four for cultivating intimacy is:

Learn to listen.

There is a simple secret that will make you interesting. I still remember the day I went to Bill Carruth, who had come to our little Texas town to teach history. He was the sharpest dresser, the wittiest and most urbane man I'd ever met, and for some reason he had taken an interest in a quiet and awkward boy.

"Mr. Carruth," I said, "I wish you could teach me how to talk with people the way you do. I can never think of anything to say."

"Loy," he replied with a wink, "the secret of being interesting is to be interested."

That simple advice has worked for me in fifty years of dealing with people—largely in public life, where I have had to meet and know thousands of individuals. When you ask questions that the other person will enjoy answering and when you encourage people to talk about themselves, an astonishing kind of connection usually occurs.

The Therapy of Listening

Patients come to counseling offices like ours because they know so few people who will genuinely listen to what they are saying. When a woman announced that she was in analysis, a church-going friend admonished her: "You have Christian friends. If you have problems, why don't you talk to them?"

"Well," she answered, "that would probably be all I'd need, if one of them would really listen to me. But do you have any idea how quickly my church friends tune me out and begin talking about themselves? It's embarrassing to have to pay for it, but to have someone give you fifty minutes of undivided attention does a world of good."

Why the Listener Is Always Popular
Because so few people genuinely attend to others, those who will learn to draw out the other person can be guaranteed all the friendships they can handle and can be assured of deepening the relationships they presently own. "The road to the heart," wrote Voltaire, "is the ear."

Dr. Carl Rogers, perhaps the foremost clinical psychologist in America in his day, said that occasionally when his patient talked on and on about deep and hidden feelings, he would suddenly notice a moistness gathering around the person's eyes, as if to say, "Thank God! At last I'm being *heard!*"

Christ was a master conversationalist. It is frequently said that he was a great teacher and healer, but his encounters with people demonstrate that he was also a remarkably attentive listener. He asked questions of lepers, Roman officers, blind men, rabbis, prostitutes, fishermen, politicians, mothers, religious zealots, invalids, and lawyers.

He was quite unusual in that quality. Many gurus and geniuses have only outgoing circuits for communication. They talk nonstop. But Jesus had incoming wires as well. He wanted to hear the men and women before him, and to know them as fully as possible.

If listening is that important, it may be helpful to tease out some of the characteristics of good listeners.

1. Good Listeners Listen with Their Eyes

According to communication experts, even when your mouth is closed you are saying a lot. When people speak to you, they are receiving many messages about how interested you are. Remember: The surest way to be interesting is to be interested, and the intensity of your interest can be measured by the way your body talks. Eye contact is one of the surest indicators. If you are staring at the wall or glancing at other people, the speaker gets a strong impression of how little you care about the conversation. On the other hand, if you look people directly in the eyes as they speak, you will be amazed at how quickly they get the compliment.

After a visit with Gordon Cosby, the eminently effective pastor of the Church of the Savior in Washington, D.C., someone said: "It's amazing the way that man listens to you. When you talk to him he seems to shut out all other interests and hang on every word you utter. It is flattering to have people give you that much of their attention."

The eye-lock is a powerful magnet for making contact with people. Dr. Julius Fast, author of *Body Language,* made a study of courting gestures and found prolonged eye contact to be the most important gesture of all. "If you hold another person's eye longer than, say, two seconds," says Dr. Fast, "it's a clear sign that you're interested."

2. Good Listeners Dispense Advice Sparingly

During the darkest hours of the Civil War, Lincoln wrote to an old friend and fellow lawyer, Leonard Swett in Springfield, asking him to come to Washington. Lincoln said he had some problems he wanted to discuss.

Swett hurried to the White House, and Lincoln talked to him for hours about the advisability of issuing a proclamation freeing the slaves. He went over all the arguments for and against such a move and then read letters and newspaper articles, some denouncing him for not freeing the slaves and others denouncing him for fear he was going to do so. After talking far into the evening, Lincoln shook hands with his old neighbor, said goodnight, and sent him back to Illinois without even asking for his opinion. Lincoln had done all the talking himself. That seemed to clarify his mind. "He seemed to feel easier after the talk," Swett said. Lincoln hadn't wanted advice. He had merely wanted a friendly, sympathetic listener to whom he could unburden himself.

Those who are experts at love are very chary of advice. When people bring you problems, they may appear to want your opinion. They may even say they need advice. But more often than not, they will thank you for simply listening. Because you help them get the problem outside themselves and on the table between you, the issues get back into perspective, and they are able to arrive at their own decision.

Especially with young people we must exercise caution that we do not stifle further conversation by offering too much advice. Philip Wylie, analyzing the gap between the generations, says:

> The fundamental complaint of [the] young . . . does not refer to the hypocrisies, lies, errors, blunders and problems they have inherited. It is, instead, this: That they cannot talk with grown people. . . . I have come to believe that the great majority of our kids have never enjoyed an intimate friendship with even one grown person. Why not? When you ask that you get one answer: Their efforts to communicate with us are invariably and completely squelched.

3. Good Listeners Never Break a Confidence

One of the signs of deepening connections with people is that they trust you with secrets. Little by little, you are handed morsels of information with which you could do them harm. Then they wait to see how you handle the trust. If you hold it gently, they breathe a sigh of relief and tell you more.

So the cardinal rule for every person who desires better relationships is: Learn to zipper your lip. Nothing causes people to clam up and to abandon your friendship more quickly than to discover that you have revealed a private matter.

If you are a leaky repository, others are sure to learn of it. When you tell one other person a fact told to you in secret, you identify yourself to the listener as an untrustworthy confidant. People do not have to be very smart to conclude that if you would tell them someone *else's* secret, you'll probably tell someone else *their* secret.

So the way to be a confidant is: Let no one know that you are a confidant to others. That is difficult for some of us, because our need for approval prompts us to show others that we are trusted by people—sometimes important people. But before long we can find ourselves trusted by no one.

An inebriated man came stumbling out of a bar and almost knocked down his minister, who happened to be walking past.

"Oh, Pastor, I'm so sorry for you to see me like this," he said.

"Well, I don't know why you should be sorry for me to see you this way, Sam. After all, the Lord sees you now, doesn't he?"

"Yeah," said the drunk, "but he's not such a blabbermouth as you are."

4. Good Listeners Complete the Loop

In their book *Mirages of Marriage,* Lederer and Jackson offer an exercise that will help you win friends and deepen your significant relationships. It is an exercise designed to help people complete the loop of communication.

Here is an example of an uncompleted loop. Husband and wife are driving along the beach. She says:

"What a beautiful sunset."

His response? Silence. Absolute quiet. What should she make of that? Silence can be described as negative feedback.

So we need to get into the habit of completing the loop. Lederer and Jackson outline three elementary steps to the exercise: Person A makes a statement. Person B acknowledges the statement. Person A confirms the acknowledgment.

For example:

Mary: Did you pick up the laundry?

Dick: No, I didn't. No parking space.

Mary: Maybe I can do it tomorrow then.

Here is another example:

Joan: I ran into Bob Bartlet today.

Gail: How is he these days?

Joan: He seemed fine.

There is a story about a young woman who was taken to dinner one night by William E. Gladstone, the distinguished British statesman, and the following night by Benjamin Disraeli, his equally distinguished opponent. Asked later what impression these two celebrated men had made on her, she replied thoughtfully: "When I left the dining room after sitting next to Mr. Gladstone, I thought he was the cleverest man in England. But after sitting next to Mr. Disraeli, I thought I was the cleverest woman in England."

5. Good Listeners Are Honored When Someone Lets Down Their Guard

Almost invariably, if people confide in you, they will be afraid of having said too much. They will be watching you carefully to see if you raise your eyebrows or appear to have lost confidence in them.

So it is important to allay those fears. As I watch people let out their closeted skeletons, I invariably feel closer to them—complimented that they have trusted me enough to divulge their secrets. So I always try to thank them. I tell them that I am honored and that their revelation does not cause me to think less of them.

It is a great gift when others trust you enough to convey information with which you could hurt them, for they took that into consideration before telling you. If you freely show your gratitude, you will open the way for even more closeness.

Again, guideline four for cultivating intimacy is:

Learn to listen.

CHAPTER 11

When Tears Are a Gift from God

I have always felt sorry for people afraid of feeling, of sentimentality, who are unable to weep with their whole heart. Because those who do not know how to weep do not know how to laugh either.
—Golda Meir

THE CRUSTY BUILDING CONTRACTOR SITTING IN A chair across from me said, "I hear everybody say that communication is supposed to be the secret of successful marriage."

"Well, it's one of them," I replied.

He glared at me. "Just what is there to talk about with a woman you've lived with for twenty-nine years?"

I smiled, trying to be sympathetic, but he didn't appear to find anything humorous in the topic.

"I know what she thinks about most stuff, we know each other's opinions on politics and religion, she's heard my stories a hundred times."

"None of your opinions ever change?"

He ignored what was doubtless a little sarcasm building up. "So when I come home at night we ask each other what we ate for lunch, and that's about it."

Conversation with your longtime friends will indeed get sparse if you restrict yourselves to facts, as that couple evidently did. But when you and your mate get together in the evening and you talk about your feelings, there will always be plenty to discuss, for every one of us has a hundred different emotions during the day. The world of our feelings is a multi-faceted, rapidly changing world, and to meet with a friend to talk about these things—that is intimacy.

Conversation can be divided into three categories: facts, opinions, and emotions. Of course, all talk contains a certain amount of all three, but you can track the degree to which two people are getting close by noticing how the talk moves from facts to opinions to emotions. New acquaintances usually restrict their conversation to facts. Then they begin to trust each other with their opinions, and finally, if they become genuine friends, emotions begin to emerge.

Here, for instance, are three ways a man can tell his office partner about lunch when he returns:

Limited to fact: "Tom and I had Reuben sandwiches for lunch today."

Including opinion: "Tom and I talked at lunch today. I really don't think his idea for changing the software is going to work."

Including emotion: "I got depressed after Tom and I had lunch today. I guess I'm jealous that the boss is listening to Tom's ideas for new software and not mine. Tom's obviously in with him these days and I'm not."

Studies show, to one's surprise, that newly married couples talk to each other more than twice as much as couples married for years. But the content of their talk is even more telling than the amount. At first, it is the sort of talk that close friends enjoy—the subjective exploring and mutual revealing of beliefs and feelings, likes and dislikes, and the trading and comparing of ideas about aesthetic subjects, sex, beliefs, and plans for the future. Later the talk is more mundane—decisions about money, household matters, problems with the children.

A married woman who, though she was not having a sexual affair, found herself falling in love with a coworker with whom she often had lunch. She mused about the difference in the way she talked to the two men in her life. "With my husband there is the office, there are the children, there are the patterns and crises of domestic days. I don't often say, 'I believe,' or 'I feel' with him. Actually, I hadn't felt the lack, so a lot of this may be my fault. But now my feelings keep multiplying, and with this new man there is a compulsion to divulge, to explain myself, to tell simple truths that lie within me."

If married people would take the effort to unravel and reveal their feelings, their evenings could be much more exciting.

Guideline number five, then, for cultivating intimacy is:

Talk freely about your feelings.

The I-Must-Always-Be-Strong Syndrome

A woman whose marriage recently ended says her friendships have a new tightness and warmth since her divorce. "I used to hear other people's troubles," she said, "but never told my own. Now that my marriage has failed right out in front of everybody, I guess I can let other things out more freely. The other day someone told me, 'I used to be put off by your superwoman act. You seem softer, more open now. I like you better this way.'"

Sometimes we develop the habit of wearing an emotional disguise because early experiences gave us the wrong start. Here, for instance, is an intelligent young woman who is unable to let herself love a man. She remains aloof and detached, and eventually all men get discouraged and leave her. In her counseling sessions we probe for memories that may have created this emotional policy. Finally it comes out. As a little girl she had more body hair than most children, and one day, when some neighbor children came over to swim, they called her "Bush."

"I started to cry," she said, "and I was so ashamed of crying that I ran into the garage and locked the door. I must have stayed in there and sobbed for half an hour, and right then and there I made up my mind that nobody was ever going to hurt me that bad again. Or see me crying again. If I cried, I'd do it alone."

The tragedy is that by so insulating herself from her emotions since, she has not only kept herself from being hurt, she has also kept herself from being loved.

Speaking at a meeting at the Beverly Wilshire Hotel, Dr. Roy Menninger, then president of the Menninger Foundation in Topeka, Kansas, explained that men are more prone than women to what he called the "I-must-always-be-strong syndrome." "The American male," said Menninger, "sees himself as a very high-powered piece of machinery rather than as a human need system."

Self-reliance is a valuable commodity and is much woven into the fabric of the American dream. But it can be carried so far that it not only makes people strong, it makes them hard. It can turn into stoicism, causing people to be isolated or appear arrogant.

Many of us were taught as children that we should not wear our emotions on our sleeves and that we should keep a stiff upper lip. I once had a client who had learned that lesson all too well. It drove him to suicide. He came to my office only twice, and I have kicked myself ever since for not seeing the severity of his pain. But outwardly there were few giveaways. About to graduate *cum laude* from an elite college, he was tall, good-looking, cheerful. His family was financing his education liberally, and he had bids from several excellent graduate schools that wanted to give him scholarships while he studied for his doctorate.

The dilemma in which he was enmeshed is a commentary on our current sexual morals as well as on his stiff-upper-lip policy. The young woman with whom he had been sleeping for several months became attracted to his best friend and began to have sex with him also. Everything was out in the open. The problem, as he presented it to

me, was not the *ménage à trois.* It was this: He felt
that a mature and urbane man should be able to
handle such a situation and he could not understand why he was jealous and upset.

Inside he was writhing with pain and rage, yet
he felt obliged to remain cheerful with his friends
and with his girlfriend, to act as if all was well, and
to keep a stiff upper lip even with me. But it was
more than the boundaries of the soul could contain, and one night he borrowed the young
woman's car, drove to a parking lot, and shot himself through the mouth. Though the suicide
occurred years ago, I think of that young man
often.

The young woman called me the day of the suicide. That weekend I met with her and their circle
of friends from school several times. Among other
things, they said, with some anger, "If only he had
let us know what he was feeling!"

Is there value to suffering in silence? Not usually. If Jesus wept freely and Abraham Lincoln was
frequently seen with tears streaming down his
face, there can be little virtue in our keeping our
emotions to ourselves. You do not show charity
for others by excluding them from your pain. As
Charles Dickens has Mr. Bumble say in *Oliver
Twist,* crying "opens the lungs, washes the counte-
nance, exercises the eyes, and softens down the
temper, so cry away."

California psychiatrist Taz W. Kinney has found
that men alcoholics outnumber women in part
because men do not cry so spontaneously. As boys
they are told to dry up their tears and be little men.
Consequently they turn to alcohol as an aid. A few

drinks provides them the license to express anger or sadness. Tears are a great gift from God—a safety valve built into our system—and there is no reason to anesthetize ourselves in order to allow them to flow freely.

Tears as a Way of Getting Close

Crying need not be a sign of weakness or an imposition on the person who witnesses it. Rather, we honor the person with whom we cry. Our tears can spring forth at moments of great joy, in the presence of beauty, or at times of sudden relief. Moreover, they can be the means by which our relationships deepen. Agnes Turnbull tells of her excitement when she was awarded an honorary degree. "As I stood to receive it," she said, "tears ran down my husband's cheeks. To think that my little moment of honor meant so much to him that he would *weep* for me!" More meaning was passed between them by his open expression of emotion than any combination of words could have carried.

The poet Robert Herrick calls tears "the noble language of the eye." If the experts are right in telling us that most communication is nonverbal, our tears, when they fall naturally, can be a powerful means of getting closer to others.

My wife, who is capable of a marvelous range of emotions, will always cry at startling good news. When I come in the door announcing that a magazine has called that day commissioning an article, she throws her arms around me and cries for a moment. Or when our heads are bowed for grace and our nine-year-old grandson tells God that he is thankful for his mother, his grandma and grandpa, and his pets, as well as the hamburgers, I can count on my wife lifting her head with a glistening in her eye. Does this quickness to cry make her unattractive? Quite the reverse. She allows me to see through to her heart when she lets me see her tears, and that elicits the strongest of loves.

Suffering Together
In the fall of 1974, the doctors at the National Naval Medical Center in Bethesda, Maryland, discovered that Betty Ford had breast cancer. On Friday she went through her appointments and duties as First Lady without making any announcement, and that evening at 5:55 the car pulled up at the Bethesda hospital. President Ford said he'd never been so lonely as he was going home to the White House that night. "He was more upset than I," Mrs. Ford writes. "I think I faced the situation rather matter-of-factly. I thought, this is one more crisis, and it will pass."

Five days after the surgery, however, she had a delayed reaction and broke into waves of weeping. Her doctor assured her it was normal postoperative depression and urged her to cry it out. But the question in her mind was how fast she could get back on her feet and return to being First Lady. When she could pick up a cup of tea with her right hand, she felt triumphant, and a week after the operation, she felt well enough to walk out to the elevator to meet her husband.

After returning home, the two celebrated their 26th wedding anniversary. She writes:

It was a fantastic anniversary. Just to be well and alive and home was wonderful. I never felt a psychic wound, I never felt hopelessly mutilated. After all, Jerry and I had been married a good many years, and our love had proved itself. I had no reason to doubt my husband. If he'd lost a leg, I wouldn't have deserted him, and I knew he wouldn't desert me because I was unfortunate enough to have had a mastectomy.

Some of Mrs. Ford's mail was from women who said that they couldn't look at their bodies after their operations, but she was curious about her scar from the minute the doctor started changing the dressing. She did worry whether she'd be able to wear her evening clothes again. "Jerry said I was silly. 'If you can't wear 'em cut low in front, wear 'em cut low in back,' he said." Their shared suffering obviously brought Betty and Jerry Ford nearer to one another.

The Swedes have a saying: "Shared joy is double joy, and shared sorrow is half-sorrow."

Remember guideline number five for cultivating intimacy:

Talk freely about your feelings.

PART III

WAYS TO HANDLE

NEGATIVE EMOTIONS

WITHOUT DESTROYING

THE RELATIONSHIP

CHAPTER 12

Being a Nice Guy Gets You Nowhere

Be angry but do not sin; do not let the sun go down on your anger.
    —Ephesians 4:26

HERE IS A MAN WE TREAT OFTEN IN PSYCHIATRIC clinics. You have known him, for he is everywhere. He may even be a member of your family. I'm referring to the "nice guy." He smiles a great deal, is cheerful with everyone, is frequently religious, never quarrels, seldom gets angry, appears to be universally liked, and might be thought to have many close friendships. But as a matter of fact, such persons can not only develop a host of psychological problems, but can also have clogged up relationships.

That may sound contradictory, for this is the fellow who doesn't have an enemy in the world.

But popularity is not synonymous with intimacy, and this man who is superficially liked by everyone is rarely loved fiercely by anyone. There are several reasons:

• He is never perceived as open. There is something about the chronically cheerful person that does not quite ring true.

• He is dull. The nice guy is pleasant to be around at first, but in the long run most of us prefer the company of people with passion. They may aggravate us at times, but at least they do not bore.

• If he cannot show anger, he is inept at showing love as well. His emotions are so tightly controlled that he has no range.

• Without knowing it, he poisons his relationships with his passive hostility.

Psychologists disagree about almost everything else, but on one point they display surprising unanimity: There is no such thing as a person who never gets angry—there are only those who suppress anger. Delaying expression of it may be necessary. But sending anger underground can produce a thousand psychosomatic problems—such as ulcers, migraines, and hypertension—as well as some serious relational difficulties.

"I Never Get Mad, I Just Get Hurt"

Passive hostility is a troublesome snake in the grass of friendship. Here is an example. Janet and Monica have opened a boutique. They have been friends for several years, but now they are partners and must work together every day. The shop opens at 10:00 A.M., and this week Janet has been late two days. Monica is annoyed, but she bites her tongue. Today Janet strolls in even later than before, after Monica has done all the work to open up the store. Janet does not apologize, and Monica is hurt. Throughout the morning she stays in the storeroom suffering in silence. She pouts, answers Janet's questions with clipped replies and gives an air of impatient aggravation. Finally Janet asks: "Are you mad or something?"

"Me? Of course not," she responds, her voice quite obviously shaking.

It is a dirty way to fight. Passively hostile people are much harder to get along with than those who express themselves with honest, direct anger. For while their behavior and their bodies are showing in a dozen ways that they have been "hurt," they are at the same time denying that anything is wrong. The result is that the acids of accumulating grudges eat away at the friendship.

Many people with passive aggression are not being dishonest when they say they are not angry—they actually may not *feel* any hostility. Their emotional control system is so well developed that anger is pushed far underground, and they do not even realize how mad they are.

The Teakettle Principle
Another destructive result of sending anger underground is that occasionally the nice guy blows up. This is something far different from normal expression of negative feelings as they occur. When we lose our temper and become unreasonable, it is usually because anger has been building up for a long time and has built up a powerful head of

steam. Finally, the teakettle ruptures. It may be an inconsiderate driver on the freeway, or it may be someone we love dearly who triggers the explosion. In any case, the steam can be very dangerous.

When the ordinarily nice guy erupts in a vicious rage, no one can understand what's wrong with him. Eventually his anger subsides, he feels terribly guilty, apologizes profusely, and returns to his passive ways of coping.

Disproportionate Anger Shorts Out Communication

When passively hostile people blow, their expression of anger is disproportionate to the complaint because they are really ventilating a lot of past grievances all at once. The result is that communication shorts out.

Keith Miller tells about feeling amorous one night and hinting to his wife in what he thought was a seductive tone of voice, "Honey, are you ready to go to bed?"

"No," she answered, "I'd like to finish this article. You go on."

So, his pride wounded, Miller went to bed alone and slept far over on his side. The next morning he came down in a nasty mood, and the toast was burnt. Suddenly an emotional dam burst. He threw the toast against the kitchen wall.

His wife noted that this behavior was a little strong for burnt toast. "But," says Miller, "the topic wasn't toast at all. The topic was sex!"

Another danger in swallowing our irritation is that our anger, when it finally erupts, is often displaced. The most common example is the husband who has had a bad day, is frustrated and irritated at his business associates, and takes it out on the dog and his family. They are all getting mail that is addressed to someone else, but they have no way of knowing that, and the family system begins to go awry.

Healthy Anger

Because aggression, frustration, and anger are emotions common to us all, the best relationships build in an allowance for negative feelings. I know of no intimate relationship of any duration that will not need to encompass some irritation and hostility from time to time, and if the two of you agree early in the friendship that occasional negativity will be welcomed, it can help enormously.

Actually, anger can be a positive force. "Men and motorcars progress by a series of internal explosions," wrote Channing Pollock. Anger can send adrenaline into the bloodstream and glycogen to fatigued muscles to restore them. Christ's eyes frequently blazed with anger, and Martin Luther said, "When I am angry I can write, pray, and preach well, for my whole temperament is quickened, my understanding sharpened, and all mundane vexations and temptations depart." That is well-managed anger.

Dr. Neil Warren, former dean of the Graduate School of Psychology at Fuller Theological Seminary, tells about his early religious upbringing, similar to that of many of us, in which he was taught that anger is sin. Jesus was presented as meek and gentle, never experiencing the emotions we do. But later, says Warren, a closer reading of the Bible revealed that Jesus was angry more than once, and, indeed, God himself does not always contain his wrath. In the Old Testament, Warren notes, there are more than 450 uses of the word "anger" (compared to about 350 uses for "love"), and fully 375 of them refer to the anger of God.

Mahatma Gandhi will always be famous for his self-sacrifice and for being a champion of pacifism. But when asked for the most creative experience of his life, Gandhi named an angry episode in Mritzburg, South Africa.

It was 1893 and Gandhi, a struggling young lawyer, was traveling to Pretoria, unaware of the unspoken prohibition against any nonwhite traveling first class. A train guard asked the little brown man to give up his compartment and occupy the baggage car. When he protested, the police constable threw Gandhi and his luggage onto the platform and the train steamed away. He made for the waiting room, which was cold and without lights. With no coat, he spent the night huddled in a corner, shivering with rage at the insult. When morning came, Gandhi had made up his mind: He would stand up for the rights of his race, cost what it might.

In reading a biography of Jefferson, I came across a line that at first seemed a wrongheaded generalization: "Jefferson, like all great men, was a great hater." Pugnacity has never been a virtue in my lexicon, but the longer I have pondered the powerful indignation that has fired the careers of men like Jefferson and Gandhi, the more I have seen the wisdom of that remark. Anger (which I would substitute for the "hate" attributed to Jefferson) can be an astonishingly creative force.

If You Dish It Out You Have to Take It

There is another side to this coin, naturally. The healthy relationship stays healthy not only because you let your negative feelings out when they occur, but also because you let your beloved do the same. Your friends are fortunate if they do not always have to be good company with you, if they can be cranky when they need to, knowing that you will not reject them for it.

It will be easier to be such a friend if you recognize that the angry outbursts of others sometimes have nothing to do with you. They are simply in a foul mood and need to drain off some of the poisons with your help. The trick is to learn to listen without making judgments about the emotions.

Managing Your Anger

The good news here is that a great deal of research has now been devoted to anger management, and it is clear that we have much more control over how we respond to stressful, tension-producing circumstances than was thought. It is possible to acknowledge our negative feelings openly and at the same time manage our actions by waiting until some of the primitive animal instincts subside and we can begin to look at an incident more rationally, using the well developed human cortex. Everyone in school studied the "flight or fight" instinct that we share with lower animals. When we hear what sounds like a huge explosion, get stepped on or shoved (either physically or emotionally), blindingly fast messages bypass the cortex and immediately set off nerves that pump adrenalin into certain areas where this primitive part of the brain assumes that it will be needed. The blood system stops sending much nourishment to the brain and stomach (thus we don't think straight at such times, and after an angry episode we often have an upset stomach). Instead, vast quantities of blood are rushed to the lungs to give us the capacity we'll need to either flee or fight and to the arms and legs for the same reason.

All this worked very well in earlier days, when human beings needed to be able to hear an attacking animal and run, or see a threatening stranger and defend themselves on the spot. However, it doesn't always serve us well now when someone cuts us off on the freeway, and we find ourselves behaving irrationally to some stranger who is of no importance whatsoever.

Shannen Doherty, a former star of *Beverly Hills, 90210,* and later one of the witches on *Charmed,* probably wished she'd been less a witch in real life when she broke a beer bottle over someone's car. She and the judge agreed that a few counseling sessions on anger management would be nice.

What she probably learned in the sessions was that the old rule of counting to ten contains some wisdom. Unless our lives actually are threatened, we need some time to allow all those physical stimulants to subside and the rational part of the brain to start functioning again. It actually takes about twenty minutes for the adrenalin to fully drain out of the system.

So if we're patient and learn to take our time, we need not be ruled by our anger.

A few people have to learn to be very cautious about venting their anger in any major quantities at any time. In therapy sessions when I was younger, I often urged clients to express anger and get their feelings out with me. "You'll feel better afterwards," I'd say. In most instances the feelings eventually subsided and it did indeed help. But with a few, I began to notice a curious phenomenon: Rather than ventilating, then having their feelings subside, the more they yelled, the more violent they became. The anger fed on itself. You know whether you are this type. If so, you will need to let out negative emotions in small portions—and thus more frequently, perhaps—and not let it get out of hand.

How to Disagree and Understand
at the Same Time

One of the surest ways to break down communication is to use the phrase often heard in serious conversation: "Please don't be so upset."

It is probably the worst possible thing to say to a friend who is in emotional trouble. Notice, for instance, what happens when we do this in marriage.

A wife comes home in a fury because a clerk has treated her rudely in a store.

"I'll never go back to that store again," she fumes, and the rage shows in every line of her body.

"Honey, don't be so upset," her husband says soothingly. "You need to remember that those clerks are poorly paid, and maybe the lady was tired at the end of the day."

What is her reaction to this attempt to make her feel better? She becomes *more* incensed because he seems to be siding with the clerk!

Her husband's aim was innocent enough. He wanted to calm her down and talk her out of her bad feelings. And he probably felt that she *was* a little unjustified in her anger and needed to see the other side.

But he failed to realize that there was no need for him to agree or disagree with his wife. She probably did not care whether he thought her feelings were justified—she merely wanted to be *heard.* But by rendering a judgment on her emotions, he made her all the more angry. What is more, he erected a wall between them, for she now felt misunderstood, one of the most painful emotions possible.

The fact of the matter is that people have a right to feel bad at times. And if we love them, we will not be hasty in trying to talk them out of their negative emotions. We'll simply give them the freedom to feel.

Dr. Edith Munger, one of my favorite therapists, knows a lot about marriage counseling. She says:

> Part of our difficulty is that we think we have to have answers for every problem our spouses raise. Actually, a personal relationship is not predicated on solutions to problems or answers to questions. Our top goal should be to understand each other, to get close to each other, experience each other. To communicate with your husband you don't have to have an answer for him. You just have to be aware of him, tasting and touching him.

The Art of Letting Them Hate You for a While
We've been discussing the virtue of accepting the negative moods of your beloved, but now we get to

a much tougher topic. What happens when someone's anger is directed at you?

That's never easy. I've never known a person who enjoyed being the brunt of another's hostility. But it will happen now and then, and it's probably healthy for the friendship if you can follow certain rules for fielding your friend's bitterness. Here are some suggestions:

Do not stifle your response. You may or may not be able to sit quietly as your beloved ventilates anger. You do not have to stifle your feelings any more than your friend does. Walter Kerr, the theater critic, would often elicit the ire of author-friends to whom he had to give bad reviews. "I could let them be mad for a while," he said. "I'd give them six months to snub me, but if they stayed mad after that, I gave myself the right to be angry back."

Do not assign permanence to emotions. It is a common trap to assume that because your friend has blasted you today, the feeling will endure tomorrow. In fact, most such emotions are transitory. The woman who says, "I'll never forget what he said to me," is only hurting herself, for once the emotion passes, the speaker will probably have no recollection of having felt it.

Remember that you can love and be angry at the same time. Most of us have a certain mixture of love and anger in all our intimate relationships, and if you will remind yourself of that fact as your loved one is railing, it may help. Charlie Shedd reports getting this note on the kitchen counter after an argument with his wife:

Dear Charlie:
I hate you.
Love, Martha.

Alternative Methods of Ventilating Your Anger

Let me make it clear that I am not here advocating the promiscuous vomiting of ill will in your important relationships. Some misinformed people go about telling everyone off because they heard some pop psychologist say that it is healthy to express anger. Not recommended. It is the part of prudence as well as charity to choose appropriate places to pronounce your displeasure. Indeed, throwing caution to the wind in getting angry may cause you to lose your job or worse. As Dean Martin used to say, "Show me a boy who has no fear, and I'll show you a boy who gets beat up a lot."

Some casual connections are simply not worth the trouble of an encounter. Walk away. In other instances, you will want to consider the time, the place, and how much damage might be done by your dumping. If your friend's self-esteem is fragile at the moment, or if your beloved is dependent on you for primary self-worth right now, you will want to move cautiously.

One way out: Ventilate your ire with a friend rather than with the person who is the irritant. If your boss is getting on your nerves, it may not be smart to blow up at him; but hopefully you have a sister or a friend or a mate who will let you fume for a while.

Alternative number two: Get some physical outlet for your aggressions. This is particularly effective for the personality type discussed above—

those who, when they talk about their anger, get more and more out of control. Certain people simply have more hostility and aggression in them than others, and it is important for such persons to get some vigorous exercise. The more competitive the better. Tennis, racquetball, punching a bag, jogging will all make you easier to get along with. Our physical well-being can have a big influence on our emotions. If you find yourself irritable and unnecessarily spouting off, it could have a solution as simple as getting more sleep or drinking less.

An old joke. Man and woman married fifty years are asked the secret of their marital bliss. "Well," drawled the old man, "the wife and I had an agreement when we first got married. The agreement was that when she was bothered about something she would just tell me off, get it out of her system. And if I was mad at her about something, I was to take a walk. I suppose you can attribute our marital success to the fact that I have largely led an outdoor life."

Let Anger Deepen the Relationship
If neither of you panic because of a few outbursts, and if you follow some of the rules for clean fighting outlined in the following chapter, it is quite possible that your friendship can be much better after the catharsis of an angry exchange. There is a certain clean feeling about restored love after a good airing of grievances. Frequently, feelings are deeper and more tender than before.

In several instances a deep friendship has begun for me after a confrontation, even after a shouting match. As we shouted at each other, finally the two of us were being authentic, we were directly experiencing the other. Then, once the problem was resolved, we were close for the first time.

When James Thurber worked for *The New Yorker,* he was at first afraid of its crotchety founder and editor, Harold Ross. Ross gave Thurber a two-week vacation the first year, and Thurber was delayed while searching for his lost dog. He returned to work two days late. Thurber says:

> Ross avoided me all day. He was in one of his God-how-I-pity-me moods. Finally he called me into his office about seven o'clock. Thunder was on his forehead and lightning in his voice.
>
> "I understand you've overstayed your vacation to look for a dog," he growled. "Seems to me that was the act of a sis."
>
> The scene that followed was brief, loud, and incoherent. I told him what he could do with his magazine, that I was through. I offered to fight him then and there, told him he had the heart of a cast iron lawn editor, and suggested that he call in one of his friends to help him. Ross hated scenes, physical violence or the threat of it, temper, and the unruly.
>
> "Who would you suggest I call in?" he demanded, the thunder clearing from his brow.
>
> "Alexander Woollcott!" I yelled, and he began laughing.
>
> His was a wonderful, room-filling laugh when it came, and this was my first experience of it. It cooled the air like summer rain. An

hour later we were having dinner together at Tony's . . . and that night was the beginning of our knowledge of each other underneath the office make-up, and of a lasting and deepening friendship.

Six Techniques to Help You Get Angry without Becoming Destructive

You and your mom have the best fights.
    —friend of a client's daughter

IS IT POSSIBLE TO "FIGHT CLEAN"? IT'S NOT ONLY possible, it's essential in solid friendships. Here are six techniques for doing so.

1. Talk About Your Feelings, Not Your Friend's Faults

Scott and Gene are roommates at school, and for the most part they are compatible. They chose to live together because they were best friends in high school and enjoyed each other's company. But the pressure builds at exam time, both get irritable, and their friendship is in trouble when this conversation occurs:

> Gene: Why do you have to wake up everybody
> in the dorm when you go to work?
>
> Scott: You think I like getting up at five in
> the morning to work in that stinking kitchen?
> Too bad my dad doesn't support me all year
> while I sit around on my can. You know, you're
> the laziest guy I know.
>
> Gene: Oh, don't give me that. Who studied
> until two this morning? I just want to know
> why you can't show a little consideration when
> you get up early.

By calling his roommate lazy, Scott went for the jugular vein rather than responding with what he felt. It is a habit many of us display when we get angry. When attacked, it is our instinct to attack back and to do damage any way we can.

To express our irritation in terms of our feelings, for which we are willing to take responsibility, does not insure protection from our friend's anger, but it is a lot less likely to wave a red flag. If Gene were to start with the following, it would at least be clean fighting:

> Gene: I gotta tell you I'm upset. Maybe I'm
> overly irritable with exams and all, but I stud-
> ied till two this morning. Then when I woke
> up when you left at five, I got bugged. I get
> bugged when it seems as if you're not trying to
> be considerate.

Scott could get defensive at this display, but he's not as likely to do so, because (a) Gene talked about what he was feeling, not what Scott had done, and (b) he tried to explain his interior state, allowing that he might be overreacting.

Here is one more illustration. If a wife says to her husband, "You never pay any attention to me anymore," it is almost certain to wave a red flag. He will respond with something like:

> What do you mean I don't pay any attention to you anymore? What about Wednesday night two weeks ago? Remember that? It doesn't seem to mean a thing to you that I take off early to take you to that ballet thing, when I've got a big lawsuit hanging over my head at work. Honestly, Helen, I don't know what it would take to make you happy. No matter what I do, you complain.

Why is he so violent? Because he has been attacked. Most of us react in such a fashion when someone says, "You never . . ." and "You always . . ."

How could she say it better? Simply by describing her feelings. Perhaps she could say, "You know, I'm really feeling lonely and neglected these days." There she is saying about the same thing as "You never pay any attention to me anymore," but note the difference: She's not accusing him of anything. She's just telling what she's feeling.

You can get away with violent feelings, even, as long as you avoid saying, "You make me so mad when you . . ." Try expressing the strongest feelings you want, but talk simply about your emotions, not what your son has done:

> Tom, I'm so mad at you I could spit nails! The later you were bringing the car back, the more frustrated I got, because I was late to my meeting. Boy, does that get to me!

It doesn't hurt to employ a little ingenuity in your negative expressions. The woman who says, "You're not very thoughtful to get up every night after dinner and march off to watch TV" isn't going to improve her relationship with her husband that way. She might put it this way: "I miss having you with me when I'm clearing the table. I'd love it if you'd keep me company until I finish with the dishes." Few husbands can say no to that kind of invitation.

2. Stick to One Topic

We can learn how to resolve interpersonal conflicts by remembering an important principle of our court system: a jury deals with the crime or crimes at hand, not the person's past. The issue becomes impossibly clouded if attorneys drag in past offenses, previous criminal records, all sorts of old issues. If you are lodging a complaint with your friend, the frustrating problem should be capable of statement in one simple sentence, such as: "It bothers me that when we have finished dinner you sit there and pick your teeth." The resolution of one problem at a time is difficult enough without pulling in old grievances.

A cooling-off period will be good if you tend to overexaggerate and overreact. And, as I've said, considerate timing will get you off to a better start. It's not the time to lodge a complaint when the person is leaving for the airport, dropping off to sleep after an exhausting day, or helping the children with homework.

3. Allow Your Friend to Respond

"You and your mom have the best fights," said a friend to my client's daughter. It had been a knock-down-drag-out session between the mother and her teenager. In fact, the fur flew so that her daughter's friend, who had been visiting, sneaked out the back door and went home.

Later she called to see if the coast was clear. She said, "I wish my mom would fight with me like that. Instead, she comes into my room, tells me off, then walks out and slams the door before I can say anything."

People who walk out during an argument are dirty fighters. If you are unhappy with someone, you have a right to express it, but you also have the responsibility to stay and hear the other side. Then there's an opportunity for resolution or compromise. But be careful not to talk for an extended period without allowing your partner's response, and do not use the old door-slamming technique as a punctuation mark.

4. Aim for Ventilation and Resolution, Not Conquest

Lots of days of pouting after a fight could be avoided if friends agreed on the ground rule that they will express their anger not to win but simply to get it out. Many people, carrying residual anger with them, will say, "Why should I tell my father about my anger? He's not going to change."

But the point is to ventilate our feelings, and hopefully search for some resolution, not to force the other to surrender. Far too many couples suppose that every time there is an argument, one or the other has to apologize. Apologies are sometimes in order and sometimes they're not. Lots of times it clears the air if the two ventilate their emotions, get their hostility out, and then go back to loving each other. No one has to conquer the other.

5. Avoid Chemicals as a Lubricant

Statistics indicate that more than half the homicides in America involve alcohol, and even if you're not thinking of mayhem, it is wise to have such discussions as these when you're clean and sober. Yes, for some people it is easier to raise an unpleasant topic after a stiff drink or two, but if you resort to that device you may do irreparable damage and not even remember what you said the next day.

6. Balance Criticism with Lots of Affection

A few years ago my friend Mark Svensson ripped into me with an uncharacteristic ferocity. He thought I was committing a major blunder, acting stupidly, and letting him and some other people down. I sat in the car and took it, but was I frosted! He was completely off base, he didn't appreciate why I had made a hard decision, and he was a poor friend to be so critical.

I went home mad and the next day I was still mad. I cancelled our regular Tuesday lunch. The following Tuesday I managed to be out of town. A few days later Mark called to see how I was. I was icy in my replies, clipped in my responses. I was still smarting from the wound.

Mark knew he had angered me, yet he felt he had no occasion to apologize (and in fact never did apologize). What he did on the telephone that day, in person the next evening, and consistently for a number of days thereafter until I was through pouting, was to gently express his affection for me. He had been genuinely indignant at what I had done, and was glad he had said so, yet he knew that it had hurt, and he understood my being miffed. It did not take many days of his affectionate displays for me to forget the whole thing.

I learned an important lesson from Mark then: You can get away with many expressions of anger if you balance them with lots of expressions of love.

PART IV

HOW TO SALVAGE

A FALTERING FRIENDSHIP

CHAPTER 14

Why Relationships Go Bad

Friendship is like money, easier made than kept.
  —Samuel Butler

THE BEST FRIENDSHIPS HAVE ALL WEATHERED
misunderstandings and trying times. Some people
assume that because they are the object of someone's wrath, the relationship is over. Not necessarily so. In fact, one of the secrets of a good connection is the ability to expect such storms. If you realize that every long-term relationship will have its
difficult times, you'll not be as likely to jump ship
when your friendship is yawing and pitching.

Fortunately, if you expect the storms, you will
also be prepared with techniques for repairing the
friendship when it goes awry. Suggestions:

1. Locate the Trouble Spot

In a therapy session an amazing conversation emerged with a man in middle-management who was depressed.

I asked a standard question: "Do you have any close friends?"

"Nope. We speak to our neighbors, but we never have anybody in."

"Why not?"

"Well, ten years ago we were real friendly with this couple. We'd play cards a couple of times a week. Even took a vacation together once. Then one week they didn't come over. My wife talked to his wife and she said it was something I'd said when we were kidding around. That was the last time we ever saw them."

His story confused me. "What did you say that offended them?" I asked.

"I have no idea."

"You mean you never asked them what had happened?" I was incredulous.

"Nope, we just dropped it there. We decided that if they were going to get upset over something like that, nuts to them."

I find that to be a sad story. Here are four people who had meant a great deal to one another, who had a very satisfactory friendship, and who had invested years in accruing good memories. And yet, because of a minor misunderstanding, the friendship disintegrated. *And the man had not taken the trouble to find out what had gone wrong.*

If your car malfunctions, you usually get it repaired. You don't junk it—your investment is too great to be able to afford that. And if you have invested heavily in a deep relationship—a friendship or a marriage—don't junk it too quickly. It probably can be fixed.

This is the diagnostic step. Look back and try to assess what has gone wrong. Where did the misunderstanding begin? How did we get into this vicious circle of put-downs?

Sometimes it's wise to do some preventive troubleshooting in your friendships. Laura Huxley makes this suggestion in her book *Between Heaven and Earth:*

> Consider a relationship which you feel could be satisfactory yet leaves much to be desired. Take the bull by the horns. Simply ask the . . . person, "What do I overlook in our relationship which is obvious to you?" Listen attentively to the answer even if you do not agree with it. Take time to think about it.

2. Apologize When You're Wrong

Maybe it worked for Ali MacGraw and Ryan O'Neal in an old movie, but I've never seen it work in real life. In *Love Story,* they conclude that love means never having to say you're sorry. Sure, it would be nice to have a love affair in which you never had to apologize, but I see a lot of spouses and friends who never say they're sorry, and that's why they end up in my office. And in many instances, so much damage has already been done that I cannot be of much help. Hosts of family problems, business partnerships in trouble, and friendships on the decline could be improved by the use of four simple words: "You may be right."

All of us are wrong—plenty of times. It is foolish to let pride and insecurity keep us from saying so and patching up the friendship. Norman Vincent Peale once wrote, "A true apology is more than just acknowledgment of a mistake. It is recognition that something you have said or done has damaged a relationship—and that you *care* enough about the relationship to want it repaired and restored."

In 1755, in the midst of an election campaign for seats in the Virginia assembly, a twenty-three-year-old colonel named George Washington said something insulting to a hot-tempered little fellow named Payne, who promptly knocked him down with a hickory stick. Soldiers rushed up to avenge the young colonel, who got to his feet just in time to tell them that he could take care of himself, thank you.

The next day he wrote Payne a letter requesting an interview at a tavern. When Payne arrived, he expected a demand for an apology and a challenge to a duel. Instead, Washington apologized for the insult that had provoked the blow, said he hoped that Payne was satisfied, and then generously offered his hand.

People who apologize are not vacillating. You must have a certain moral certitude to admit you are wrong. Because relationships are the most difficult things we attempt in this life, of *course* we will make mistakes in them. And when we do, we can save ourselves considerable misery by apologizing.

3. Check to See If Your Neuroses Are Spoiling Your Friendships

If your relationships seem to be shorting out regularly, you might do well to ask if your neurotic patterns of relating are causing the problem.

For instance, we sometimes see others through the filter of past memories. A person reminds us of someone we once knew, or we get flashbacks to some failure in a similar relationship. For several months I saw a widow of thirty-one. She was tall and graceful, with sparkling brown eyes, and she exuded vibrancy every time she moved her lithe body. She was witty and threw her head back to laugh every few minutes during the sessions. She was far above average in intelligence and had a responsible job at which she made plenty of money.

But where did all these attributes get her with men? Nowhere. She had no trouble attracting men, of course, and she desperately wanted to marry again. But inevitably she found herself doing and saying things that turned the men off. They would leave her, and she would go through another period of mourning.

As we tried to sort out the strands that were causing so much difficulty, she began to remember and relive the terrible events surrounding her husband's accidental death. When she had arrived at the accident scene, his body had not yet been moved, waiting for a medical examiner. When the firemen pulled back the cover for her to identify his body, his limbs were akimbo, his cuts still oozing blood. He was virtually naked, his clothing cut away when the paramedics had tried to revive him. All this material was so distasteful and tragic that she had suppressed it from her conscious memory. When we uncovered her past—as gently as I knew how—she sobbed over it sometimes and raged over it at others. But as we looked at this bundle of emotions, she began to see what an inner civil war she had been housing, and she recognized the havoc these memories were creating when she was with men. At one level she wanted to be married, but at another level she was frightened at the prospect of losing her man again. So her unconscious solved the problem by causing her to be repulsed even at the sight of a man's body, which new men picked up on quickly.

When she began to see what her unconscious was doing, she developed ways of dealing with the present, uncontaminated by the past. Soon she began to function normally on dates, and has now been happily married for some time.

Several years ago I took on another client with the same problem relating to others because of the past, but in this instance, she couldn't trust women. It didn't take any complicated psychoanalysis to see where her distrust originated. Her mother had been a chronic alcoholic, unavailable to her much of the time during her childhood. When sober, her mother was often hungover and irritable. At other times she criticized the little girl and punished her in the cruelest ways. The girl was thin and had a poor appetite. When she did not eat her meals to her mother's satisfaction, the mother put a plywood screen on the table around her and her plate so she would not be distracted by the other children at the table. If she *still* would not eat, her mother would leave her sitting there picking over the cold food, even after the rest of the family had gone to bed.

My client was not a good student as a girl, and the parents, both of whom were intellectuals, berated her for her stupidity. They took her to psychiatrists (who concluded she was not mentally ill, but simply possessed an average IQ), and in general so tore away at her self-esteem that she had become a timid bundle of fears who pleadingly looked to me for encouragement each week. She clung to the emotional nourishment I tried to give her as if she were a starving child in Calcutta.

That was doubtless because I am male. From women she did not even dare to hope for love. Her past was still too much with her. How did she compensate? Because she had no fear of men, she connected sexually with a string of men because it brought her at least temporary self-assurance.

Therapy with this woman was long and difficult for me, because she needed so much. But I kept reminding myself that it was far tougher for her than for me, and that I must stay with her, however long it took, until she had enough good data from present relationships that she could stop expecting them to backfire, and stop compensating by seducing men.

I would like to report that this client was quickly cured, but her inability to trust others, especially women, has not yet gone away entirely. Her work has taken years. But she has finally gained the courage to begin working with a female therapist, and she is getting better.

Why is one child so traumatized by a harsh childhood and others endure even harsher ones and emerge into adulthood functioning well and leading a normal life? I wish I knew. That is still a great mystery to me. So I do not grind on the conundrum unnecessarily; I have my hands full trying to help my clients identify and correct their distortions.

4. Check to See If You Employ Old Methods of Relating That No Longer Work

Each of us has a craving for emotional nurture, and along the way each of us has acquired a bagful of tricks for getting it. Unfortunately, we can learn some very neurotic ways of doing so, and those patterns can get us into trouble again and again.

A man I know grew up in a home that was stable enough, but little love was dispensed, either verbally or physically—except when he was sick. When he or his sister were ill, their mother became quite affectionate, hovered over them, got up during the night to tuck them in, and gave them lots of special attention.

A child desperately wants strokes and will go to almost any lengths to get them. In this case the method was simple enough: Get sick a lot. It was not that the boy pretended to be sick. He found himself coming down with colds and fevers anytime he felt insecure or under pressure and needed some extra love. It was a skewed method of getting strokes, but it worked.

Then the boy married. Naturally he took into his marriage most of the relational patterns he had learned at home, including the get-sick-when-you-need-love trick. He assumed that this new woman would respond in the same ways as the old one.

But there was a catch. His wife was never sick herself, didn't like to have anything to do with sickness, and had a certain disdain for people who babied themselves when they had a cold or fever. So, when he came down with the old illnesses, she gave him *less* attention instead of more. Yet the poor fellow, operating with devices that he'd unwittingly learned from childhood, continued to ask for love by running a fever or catching a terrible cold. And it continued to backfire.

It wasn't until years later, and after much damage to the marriage, that the husband discovered how his psychosomatic problems were causing him difficulty, why he had developed them in the first place, and how he could exchange them for a more direct and successful way of soliciting his wife's love.

Your tricks may not be the same as this man's, but survey your relationships to see if old neurotic patterns, which once worked with someone else, have now become counterproductive.

Creative Forgiveness

*Lord, when we are wrong, make us willing to change,
and when we are right, make us easy to live with.*
   —Peter Marshall

IT WILL BE APPARENT BY THIS TIME THAT I BELIEVE
strongly in reconciliation—that faltering relationships can usually be salvaged. Occasionally you
realize you're in a poisonous one, where for your
sanity you must withdraw, but most often, broken
relationships stay broken for the lack of a patience
that will let the other person go through a period
of temporary insanity.

I certainly have never been known for the sta-
bility of my moods. One reason my partnership
with Taz W. Kinney, M.D., never faltered was that
Taz would patiently allow me these irregularities.
He'd say to the office staff, "McGinnis is gone for a

while. He's in one of his moods, and we're going to have to take up some of the slack for him. But he'll be back. Later I'll be temporarily insane, and *he'll* be carrying things."

Who could keep from having a good business partnership and friendship with such a man?

Sometimes it is in the nature of intense relationships to create conflict. When one compares Thomas Jefferson's gravely formal and almost life-long correspondence with James Madison (with whom he never quarreled) to his sparkling, sometimes contentious letters to John Adams, it is apparent that he loved Adams far more than Madison. And yet the famous friendship between Jefferson and Adams was interrupted by eleven years of bitter silence. Both were unhappy to be estranged, but the thaw occurred very slowly. Benjamin Rush knew the two men well, and he recognized that they both longed for reunion, so he carried information back and forth between them until finally they agreed to resume correspondence. In the next fourteen years, until both men died July 4, 1826, many warm exchanges occurred between them—what one historian has called the richest exchange of letters in American politics.

Mark Svensson grew up in the city of Udvala on the western coast of Sweden, and often told me about spending summer days with his Aunt Ellen, who lived a twenty-minute walk away.

"Aunt Ellen was a strange one," Mark said, "but I loved her anyhow. As a girl, she had been in love with my father, so when he married one of her sisters—my mother—she decided to kill herself. The suicide she chose was to jump from the second-story window of a very low-slung house. She landed in the gooseberry bush."

"Did she break anything?" I asked.

"Only the bush."

"Was she a spinster all her life?"

"Yes," Mark replied. "Maybe by choice, but probably without much choice. She supported herself by cleaning a church and working as a seamstress, but made so little that she had to live with her brother all her life. They weren't all that compatible. She was a Rosicrucian and a Nazi who told everyone she wanted Hitler to win the war. The fact that her brother and his wife were Pentecostals and had home prayer meetings accompanied by considerable noise praising God must have irritated Aunt Ellen, because she was a very irritable lady."

"If she was so irritable, why did you spend so much time with her?" I asked.

"Well, I was her favorite nephew, and she doted on me as a little boy, and I learned to follow her rules. For instance, when I visited Aunt Ellen, I could never speak to Aunt Selma though she would be there in the same house. I had to choose."

"Why?"

"Because Aunt Selma and Aunt Ellen had had a falling out over something, and neither would give in. They shared the same cramped little kitchen for forty years but they never got back on speaking terms. So far as I know, neither said a word to the other for forty years."

Most people have stories of grudges and feuds in their families—though few are as risible as Mark's—and most of us need some skill in the art of forgiveness so we can avoid such long-term standoffs.

Forgiveness As a Positive Force

The forgiving person is sometimes caricatured as weak and spineless, but the opposite is true. One must be strong to forgive, for forgiveness is a very positive force. It changes both you and your beloved.

The sad thing about hate, on the other hand, is what it can do to the hater. I talked with a young mother who was bristling with bitterness. Her husband's parents had said some unkind things to her, there had been a bad scene, and she told me, "I'll never feel the same toward my in-laws again. They've apologized, but I can't forget what they said."

I felt sorry for that woman, for she was the one who was suffering most from her hatred, not her in-laws. In fact, the dangerous thing about bitterness, slander, wrangling, malice, and the whole cargo that St. Paul urges us to jettison (Eph. 4:31-32) is that these attitudes eat away at us like acid. Not only does our bitterness slop out on those around us and corrode our relationships, it also eats away at our own souls.

A friend of Clara Barton, founder of the American Red Cross, once reminded her of an especially cruel thing that someone had done to her years before. But Miss Barton seemed not to recall it.

"Don't you remember it?" her friend asked.

"No, I distinctly remember forgetting it."

You can't be free and happy if you harbor grudges, so put them away. Get rid of them. Collect postage stamps or movie posters or coins, if you wish, but don't collect grudges.

Just as bitterness produces more bitterness, so love begets love. Thank God for those dynamic, creative people who, when wronged, refuse to compound the amount of hate in the world. Instead of returning the blow, they forgive.

When I was in graduate school, we lived in a low-rent area of Los Angeles where there were many children, some of them from poor homes. The only place they had to play was in the street, and I'd stop to talk with the boys and girls often. One day a sunny little voice behind me said, "Hello, Mr. McGinnis."

I turned around and saw a little mass of freckles seven or eight years old. She came wobbling up the sidewalk on her brother's bicycle. She was wearing a swimsuit and licking a Popsicle. Her eyes were as blue as Santa Monica Bay. She swung one leg down to stop her bike, and I said, "Hi, Punky. I haven't seen you around for several days."

"I've been on a trip."

"Where'd you go?"

"I went to Santa Barbara to see my mother for two weeks. She moved away, and I don't live with her anymore."

I winced, wondering how a mother could leave such a sunny little girl. I don't know, of course, how that mother's life has been disarranged, and perhaps her circumstances are beyond her control. *But doesn't she realize how bitter her daughter is going to be?*

Then I had to stop myself as I watched Punky wobbling away, happily licking her Popsicle, for I realized: *She's not bitter. She's been dealt a blow she didn't ask for and didn't deserve, but she's not passing on the blow. She's passing on happiness and sunlight. She stopped to say "Hello, Mr. McGinnis," and to tell me about her trip. And if she can continue to go through life without holding grudges, passing on a smile in return for a blow, she'll become a beautiful and charming woman.*

Being the First to Bury the Hatchet

If we forgive positively, we'll take the initiative in forgiving. I find this to be very difficult to do. If someone apologizes, then I'm usually willing to let bygones be bygones, but it's harder when I've been wronged (or think I have) and my enemies don't even admit their errors.

What about the obnoxious person who never says "I'm sorry"? Here we can profit by noticing how it is that God forgives us. The startling thing about divine love is that God did not wait until we had apologized to send his Son. He took the initiative. He took the first step. "While we still were sinners Christ died for us" (Rom. 5:8). That is, he did not wait until we were repentant, until we had shaped up, until we had changed our ways. Had he waited, of course, we never would have repented. But because he forgave us when we did not deserve it nor even ask for it—*that* caught us short.

When you have been loved in such a fashion, you want to change. Think for a moment about the people who have influenced you for the better, who have brought out the best in you. Aren't they the ones who have taken the initiative with you, believed in you, and forgiven your faults? Then, because they accepted you as you were, you wanted to change.

In James Hilton's novel *Goodbye, Mr. Chips,* the hero is a shy, inept schoolteacher, bungling and unattractive in a dozen different ways. And then something happens. He meets a woman who loves him and whom he loves, and they are married. And because of her he turns into a kind, gracious, friendly man—so much so, in fact, that he becomes the most beloved teacher in the school. There is a positive, potential power in love.

What did St. Paul mean in his great hymn to love when he wrote, "love does not keep a record of wrongs" (1 Cor. 13:5 TEV)? I think he meant that to love we must be able to believe that people's characters do alter, that the leopard *can* change its spots, that conversions do occur, that people do repent, and that at times they do change. To put it another way, he was urging that when we are in relationships of long standing we must live in the present, forgetting some of the slights we've endured in the past. For sooner or later, in any friendship, someone will be wronged. In a weak moment, the beloved will severely criticize or embarrass, or temporarily walk away. If we allow ourselves to dwell on those misdeeds, the relationship is doomed. Keeping close books on how many wrongs have been done us makes us accusatory. It is curious what a short memory we have for our own mistakes, and what a long one we have for the mistakes of others.

If we are to forgive freely, we need a tolerance of others as generous as that tolerance we display toward our own errors. Someone has said that we judge others for what they did and ourselves for what we intended—we didn't intend the error, or it happened in a moment of stress, or we weren't feeling right that day, or we'll know better next time. We tend to see ourselves not for our current behavior but for what we are striving to be, whereas we see others simply for their behavior. Jesus, in his encounters with people such as Peter and the woman at the well, saw them for what they were trying to become and what they would eventually be. To extend such understanding toward our intimates can do a great deal to build strong friendships.

Forgiving Proportionately

If you set out to develop more understanding toward other people it will help to recall how generously we have been forgiven by God. General Oglethorpe once said to John Wesley, "I never forgive and I never forget." To which Wesley responded, "Then sir, I hope you never sin." Very apt, for when we reflect on how much God has forgiven us, it makes our own little grudges against others seem rather petty.

It can be transforming to pray the Lord's prayer with its request for help in forgiving. A stockbroker, whom I will call Clarence, tells about having a falling-out with another broker in the same office. They had a dispute over a client, and after that, though they passed each other's desk every day, they did not speak. One day in church, as Clarence was praying the Lord's Prayer, he came to: "Forgive us our debts, as we also have forgiven our debtors" (Matt. 6:12). "There was no question in my mind," he says, "who was in the wrong and who owed who. *Sam* had been in the wrong when he took my client away from me! But it wasn't right for us not to be speaking, and I had to do something.

"While the others were repeating the rest of the prayer, I asked God to help me with Sam. The next afternoon, when the market had closed and I was finishing up some papers, I breathed another prayer and went over to Sam's desk and said, 'You know, Sam, you used to tell me about the trouble your wife was having with arthritis, and I've been wondering how she's getting along.'

"Sam looked startled at first, but then words began to tumble out—how they'd had her to three specialists in the past year, and that she was a little better, thank you. And as we talked he told about taking a walk together for two blocks the night before, which was pretty good. And among other things, he said that he was too quick with his tongue and often did things he didn't mean to do. Though he didn't come out and say it, I knew that was Sam's way of apologizing.

"And the next morning when he came by my desk, he said, just like he used to, 'Good morning, Clarence!' And I said, just like I used to, 'Good morning, Sam!'"

Forgiving Prayerfully

There is one more thing. In the last analysis, we need divine power to help us forget. No matter how much we want to be Christ-like and patient, no matter how hard we try to keep our emotions under control, the bitterness and revenge in us sometimes erupt and the hot lava of our rage spills out. We must have help from God. Surely it is not by accident that Christ urges us to pray for those who persecute us, because amazing things happen when we pray for our enemies.

I talked with a young man who had recently made a decision of faith and had turned the controls of his life over to God. He had grown up an orphan, his opportunities had been narrow, and he had a chip on his shoulder. "I could never get along with my bosses," he said, "and I especially despised my foreman. He seemed to have it in for me, and I was itching for revenge. But because I was now trying to be a Christian, I decided to start praying every day. I prayed for my family, and I prayed for my neighbors, and then I gritted my teeth and prayed for the foreman. And do you know, when I started doing that, something happened to that guy! It wasn't but a few weeks until he had changed so, and now we're pretty good friends.

"Of course," he smiled, "I guess I was the one who changed."

God can change you if you will ask him. If the memory system of your mind has stored up bitterness and revenge and malice, Christ wants to come in and erase that for you and give you love.

Christ is something of an expert on the art of forgiving. It was he who said, "Father, forgive them; for they know not what they do."

PART V

COMMITMENT

CHAPTER 16

Loyalty— The Essential Ingredient

A friend is one who walks in when others walk out.
  —Walter Winchell

I OCCASIONALLY DRIVE TO VALYERMO, IN THE DESERT, where a Benedictine monastery nestles up against the north face of the San Gabriel Mountains. The food is good there, there are no telephones in the rooms, and I have a chance to take long walks among the Joshua trees.

And at meals the conversation is good. The brothers of St. Andrew's are remarkably well educated. Several have doctorates from such places as Harvard, Louvain, the Sorbonne. Another is an M.D. from UCLA.

One day at lunch I sat across from Father Eleutherius. He is a tall, ascetic man who for many years drove a hundred miles once a week to lecture to students in philosophy at Claremont Graduate School. He is famous for his erudite works on philosophy, all in French. His mind was occupied with other things that day, and he did not have much to say as we ate until he learned that I was writing a book on friendship. His eyes came alive, and he said, "Ah, friendship!"

Then he paused a long while, pondering. His face saddened and he said, "It's unfortunate that friendship is so little cherished in America. My true friends are not here, but one in India, and the other in Belgium. By that I mean that we have a certain loyalty to one another. I am devoted to them, and they to me."

Loyalty. Devotion. Those are haunting words from an older era, largely lost from our vocabulary.

The Beauty of Lifelong Relationships

Those who are rich in their friendships seem to be those who believe in lifelong relationships, who stay with their companions through thick and thin, who weather the dry spells.

My father was seventy-three when his best friend died. His grief at Hubert's death made me realize what their friendship had meant to them for more than sixty-five years. They had grown up as boys in the same rural town, had fished and hunted together as both boys and adults, and had never lived more than six miles from each other. My father, reflecting on their similarities, said: "Well, Hubert and I had a lot in common. Margaret and your mother were the only girls either of us ever went out with, and we stayed married to them for more than fifty years."

At times the two men did not see much of each other because one or both were very busy, but there were hidden sinews of loyalty there. Hubert always sent a bushel of oranges to our house in the fall when his orchard was bearing, and my father would drop by Hubert's nursery, where they would have long talks as they walked among the rows of shrubs. They were in the same adult Sunday school class for nearly half a century.

Constancy

There are people who are chronic failures at all their intimate relations and who are always on the move—lurching from one marriage to the next, from one friendship and into another, thinking all the time that the trouble has been with their friends. They suppose that their hope for happiness lies in finding better people somewhere in the world. Often estranged from their relatives, they also carry on feuds with their neighbors and coworkers. But sooner or later, you must learn to hang on when the going is tough.

Today's divorce laws have made it easy to dissolve marriages, but does anyone suppose that people are on the whole happier today with their serial marriages than a hundred years ago when people stuck together in so-called unhappy marriages? From my experience it seems that most people who are unhappy and discontent with their partners will be equally unhappy and discontent with the partners of a second marriage.

I am not judging or criticizing those who have to get out of a destructive marriage. Once in a while it turns out to be necessary for survival. Yet I think there is good reason for the Bible's strong stand on the permanence of marriage and on divorce as a manifestation of our sinfulness.

In most durable friendships, the glue that has held them together is the commitment we've been discussing. Let me illustrate. I meet with a group of seven men every fortnight who talk about our thoughts and feelings and then pray for one another. These men are all strong leaders—pastors of large churches or bold, aggressive doctors. When people such as these meet regularly, month in and month out, a certain amount of competitiveness is inevitable, and we sometimes grate on one another's nerves.

One man, a very successful scientist and physician, possesses by far the strongest intellect among us and finds it easy to grab the conversation and run off on hobby horses without considering the others. Since the purpose of our meeting is not to discuss intellectual issues, my friend routinely gets tackled when he is about five minutes into these monologues and barely warmed up. At times we have been so hard on him that I have felt guilty when the meeting was over and wondered if he would be back.

But here is a wonderful thing—the man never stays away because we have been critical. Doubtless he would just as soon find something else to do some weeks, but he is a man who abides by his commitments. He had made a pact with us that we would link arms and support one another as Christian brothers, and though at times the relationships have produced sparks, he has not flinched nor fled.

The result? That man is a fast friend to each of us, and there is little that we would not do for him. He says now that he has never had companionship such as the seven of us enjoy together, that we are his best friends. And he is right—we love him dearly and perhaps are all the more loyal to him because of the way he has weathered our beatings, listened to our reactions, and worked the complicated connections through.

On Giving Up Too Easily

In any permanent relationship, there are going to be periods when your friend is not functioning well and consequently the friendship is not functioning well. The test is whether you can stay and wait.

All of us, at one time or another, have such periods. A fine line divides our normal coping with reality and our slipping into some unreality. And all of us cross over it occasionally. For most of us it occurs briefly—perhaps for less than a day—and a good night's sleep is its cure. But others have periods when they need the support and guidance of people who love them.

I have been able to be much more understanding of my clients' bouts with irrationality since experiencing it myself. After a sleepless night a few years ago, I found myself out of control. The next several months were a living hell. I probably will never fully understand all the causes for that rocky period. Whatever the reasons, I could not cope, and I will always be grateful for a few people, mostly members of my church, who held me up. After a few months, I regained my equilibrium and returned to normalcy.

That is what's significant: People almost always get over their periods of instability. The loss of control is temporary. Given some quietness, it is likely that our minds will heal and we will be all right soon.

Harry Emerson Fosdick, who later became the nationally famous pastor of Riverside Church in New York City, had a full-fledged break while in seminary. After a few days and nights of agonizing tension, he fled to his family in Buffalo and was not able to return to school until the following year.

Today we would prescribe medications for such a person quickly—perhaps too quickly. But, of course, the anti-psychotics were not available then. How did Fosdick recover? With time, primarily. And with the understanding support of his fiancée and parents. Eventually the tide would turn, but for months he despaired of ever returning to normalcy and was on the verge of suicide. Writing almost fifty years later about his journey into darkness, Fosdick said that he learned things about God then that seminaries never teach. He learned to pray, and he learned the power of a few loved ones who do not walk out when you are at your worst.

It is sobering to consider what might have happened if Fosdick's family had decided that he was hopelessly crazy and given up on him. The church would have been deprived of one of its great leaders.

What I am arguing for here is perseverance in human relationships, for a stick-to-it-iveness that will keep you connected until that stretch of road is in your rearview mirror. Then the relationships that were once good can be good again.

The demand for complete reciprocity all the time can hurt a friendship. Glenn and George have been close since they were coworkers in the same company ten years ago. They have gone on to new jobs but continue to have much in common, and until recently saw one another regularly. But Glenn was recently promoted to a top managerial job with lots of money, lots of stress, and a country club membership that he is expected to use. George tells himself he doesn't envy Glenn and wouldn't have his job for a minute. Yet he feels that Glenn's new prestige has gone to his head a little, and he resents that Glenn says he has no time for the fishing trips they once enjoyed.

It probably is true that for the first few months, Glenn's new job is occupying all his emotional attention. If George carried a scale around to weigh the give-and-take in the friendship, he could demonstrate that he is giving more than he is getting from Glenn. But fortunately George is fairly relaxed and possesses a lot of patience. They have been friends long enough that he does not fear that Glenn is trying to dump him—his mind is simply filled with other things now. Their relationship will be better later, and in the meantime he is willing to accept the reduced amount of reciprocity in the friendship.

George is wise, for in all relationships there is a movement. It is like a dance—at times moving toward each other, and at other times apart. The secure friend does not panic during a phase of withdrawal.

Looking Out for Number One?

The self-help industry seems capable of cranking out an endless supply of books, tapes, and seminars that advocate believing in yourself, tapping the unlimited power within yourself, asserting yourself, competing confidently, taking advantage of the other person before the other person takes advantage of you, and telling anyone who does not give you what you want to get lost.

Actually, these movements are not entirely new. Arrogance has been around for some time.

But there is a pathos to such a philosophy of living. It is the attempt of unhappy people to find some joy for themselves. Someone has told them that they will find it by ignoring the people around them and elbowing their way to the front of the line. But my experience in counseling such people is that when they push others away, intimidate their competitors, and disregard those to whom they have responsibility, they get to the front of the line and discover that there is no one there to hand them any prizes. Jesus dismissed such a way of living, saying that those who save their lives will end up losing them.

Christ also said that those who lose their lives will save them, and the Bible is replete with statements to the effect that sacrificing ourselves and denying ourselves for some higher good will in the long run bring happiness. In other words, happiness does not ordinarily come to those who set out to "be happy."

I notice that the most fulfilled people do not have to shove and push. They do not worry about intimidating others; they have a certain confidence that comes from giving to others. There are rewards for such acts, for the friend who is willing to sacrifice for you is not easily forgotten. More about this will follow in later chapters.

Here is a woman whose husband has lost his job and his self-confidence. He is a bear to live with, and he has become impotent for the first time in his life. Money is scarce. She clearly is not getting much from the marriage. The aggressive woman, who is looking out for number one, might begin to think about dumping him. But not this understanding, patient person, who believes in the value of lifelong commitments to those she loves and recognizes that her husband relies on her now as never before and that there are periods in any relationship when one does most of the giving.

There is something about the inherent goodness of her loving that will always cause her to be profoundly loved by those around her. And who knows? In a few years she may meet with a serious setback herself, and will require something in the bank.

And what of the mothers and fathers who have nursed their handicapped children for a lifetime? Are we to say that they were foolishly uninformed to put up with so much bother, that they should have known about looking out for number one?

I am talking to a forty-year-old woman whose aged parents are her responsibility, and I am concerned that perhaps she is too tied to them, that she is giving too much.

"Oh, I don't think so," she answers.

"But do you *enjoy* taking them to the doctors, and all those chores?" I persist. I suspect weak ego strength and am probing, without telling her, for telltale signs that she enjoys punishing herself.

She looks at me as if I should find some other line of work. Then her reply is filled with much common sense and generosity.

"Enjoy it? Well, not if you mean pleasure in the event. Who likes sitting in doctors' offices for two hours waiting for them to spend two minutes examining your mother and another two to say that her back pain is nothing but arthritis, that she is getting old and should expect those things?

"But if by enjoy it, you mean that I get satisfaction from it, yes, I do. Lots of satisfaction. My parents gave to me for so long, when I'm afraid I didn't give them much gratitude. Not much of anything except demands. When you're young you don't think.

"So now if I can do some things for Mom and Dad, it makes me feel good. Sure, I would rather be talking to somebody else for an afternoon—I've heard Pop's stories so often, and he gets so excited and so unreasonable when he talks politics. I blow up at them sometimes when it gets unbearable.

"But they have loved me for forty years, and I figure it's not going to hurt me to tough it out a while for them. Which is a roundabout way of saying that I love my parents very, very much."

She is in a long line of people who seem to have little time to worry about peak experiences for themselves—people who find their joy by investing themselves in others.

The motivation for many such magnanimous acts has for two thousand years come from a rabbi from Nazareth who, his witnesses said, "went about doing good." Not only did he leave a large body of teachings on the value of love, which does not seek its own—he was also the embodiment of such love. When all is said and done, Christ is our teacher on the art of relating.

From the first time we see him, at the age of twelve, in relationships, he is surrounded by persons with whom he forges a strong link. He opens himself in a remarkable way to a number of intimates, and again and again we see him extending himself to take the initiative in loving others, doing favors for strangers, defending the disadvantaged, risking himself for others when there is no possibility that he will ever reap anything from them.

Jesus, of course, had divine self-confidence. It was so strong that he did not have to prove himself in every verbal contest or battle for power. Instead, Christ expressed gentleness and generosity. His was a love that transformed a dusty little province of the Roman Empire into the Holy Land simply because he walked there.

All of this is not to say that Christ was passive. His lack of aggressiveness does not mean that at all. The lovers of this world are the strong ones. They are the builders. They are the creators. For rather than compounding the amount of hate in the world, they compound the amount of charity.

CHAPTER 17

Rejection and Its Aftermaths

I just keep goin' up there and swingin' at 'em.
  —Babe Ruth

HER NAME WAS CASSIE. HER BEAUTY HAD BEGUN to fade, but her eyes sparkled and her bearing was genteel. As we became acquainted, I realized that the air of self-confidence was a facade, and she seemed more and more like a frightened bird. Her marriage had ended in divorce a decade ago. One or two friendships with women had also gone awry, so she decided to withdraw. She had lived in almost total isolation for ten years. Her dealings with people at work, the supermarket, the gas station, and the cleaners were all friendly, but she spent her evenings half-watching television. She related deeply to no one. Finally, here she was in my office, for no one can survive such isolation.

Cassie has many twins—people who are lacking in love because they have chosen isolation. Hurt by the failure of some friendship, they have concluded that they cannot or should not attempt another intimate connection.

Divorce and Its Aftermath

If there is a single incident in our adult lives likely to discourage us about relationships, it is divorce. Each year more than a million and a half Americans dissolve their marriages, and when these statistics are examined in more detail, they reveal that one of every nine adults has been traumatized by it.

The outside observer might suppose that, human nature being what it is, all these divorced people would blame their partners for the failure. But as we discussed earlier, an entire group exists for whom the opposite is true. Many people in my acquaintance blame themselves more than their former mates. It's true that the people I see may have lower self-esteem than other divorced persons, because they're in counseling, but in several instances I have worked with both the husband and wife after their marriage ended. I found that *both* blamed themselves unreasonably. Neither felt capable of loving or being loved and neither was dating.

It would of course be arrogant to go blithely on one's way after such an event as if one had *no* responsibility for the tragedy. On the other hand, it is lamentable when a person comes ducking out of a failed marriage, convinced that no future relationship is going to work.

At all costs, you must not withdraw because a marriage has failed. During that time of stress you need friends and family as never before, and if you let them nurse you for a while, you will find your ability to love returning.

One of the pleasures of my work is seeing that happen. A man comes in for an initial visit with no energy, no enthusiasm, no self-confidence, the anguish showing in every line of his face. His wife has informed him that she is sleeping with someone else and is leaving.

But he works hard at therapy and as our sessions go along this battered man begins to regroup. Vivacity and vitality return. He begins to laugh. And then one day he tells me about a woman he has met. They're not rushing into anything, but she treats him so well.

A bonus in being a therapist is that Diane and I get to attend a lot of happy weddings.

The Freedom to Fail

To succeed at intimate relationships (and at all other enterprises, actually), you need a certain freedom to fail. Most experts at friendship have gone through a few ruptured relationships that remained broken, and they realize that it will happen again. They do their best to prevent it, and to provide good maintenance for their current friendships and family connections, but if something goes wrong, they do not automatically assume that something is wrong with *them*. Friendships, like plants, can die natural deaths. People move away from others in interests and inclinations. There is a certain attrition in all things. Lifelong relationships may be wonderful, but they are quite rare. When we have had a good friendship for a few months or a few years, we can be grateful for the time we had together rather than lamenting that it did not last forever.

The Mark of Success—Ability to Handle Rejection
In Atlanta, I once talked to a sales manager who had coached some of the most successful and best-paid marketing executives in the business.

"Do you know the telltale sign that people will be excellent in sales?" he asked.

I guessed. "Intelligence? Ambition? Drive?"

All were wrong.

"It's their ability to handle rejection. If they are cowed by failure with a few customers, they'll never hit the big time. But if they can endure rejection and keep trying, confident that they will eventually find a customer where everything clicks, there's no stopping those kinds of people."

The same principle works in our close relationships. Our ability to discover love will in part depend on our ability to handle turned backs and closed doors. Occasionally someone will spurn us. When we initiate a friendship and the other does not wish it, that rejection can burn through many lines of defense.

But the inescapable fact is that not everyone will like you. When they do not, it is not necessarily a reflection on you. The chemistry simply is not right. Not even Jesus was universally loved. In fact, he made a number of enemies, and it probably follows that if you attempt a worthwhile life, you will have enemies as well. Rollo May somewhere says that one of the advantages of living in a small town is that you learn to live with your enemies, and indeed it is a worthwhile lesson to discover that though a few people will dislike you, you can still have more close friends than you can handle.

The Joy of New Friends

Even Samuel Johnson, that most clubbable of men, recognized that his friendships were constantly shifting. Hence his celebrated remark: "A man, sir, must keep his friendships in constant repair. If a man does not make new acquaintances as he advances through life, he will soon find himself left alone."

Paul Tournier, at age seventy-five, noted that one of the joys of his superannuation was that most of his and his wife's friends were younger than they:

> Sometimes one hears it said that it is not easy to form new friendships once one is no longer young. If this were really the case, my luck would be exceptional. My closest friends from the period of my childhood and youth are nearly all dead and gone. My wife, too, has lost many of hers. But we have lots of new friendships, wonderful friendships with men and women who are mostly younger than we, and who certainly play their part in keeping us young in heart and mind. Some of our closest friends we have known for only a few years.

To Have an Amplitude of Friends, Keep Trying

It is seldom noted that Babe Ruth missed and missed and missed the ball. In fact, he struck out 1,330 times, a record in futility un-approached by any other player in baseball up to that time. But what people remember is that he hit 714 home runs, a record unequalled for decades. Someone once asked Ruth the secret of his success at the plate. "I just keep goin' up there and swingin' at 'em," he replied.

PART VI

IDENTITY AND INTIMACY

CHAPTER **18**

Why Subservience Is Always Dangerous

The paradox of love is that it is the highest degree of awareness of the self as a person and the highest degree of absorption in the other.
　—Rollo May

"IF I EVER GET MARRIED AGAIN," HE SAID, "I'M GOING to Japan to find a geisha-type woman. What I want is a wife who's to live for nothing more than to please her man."

He was half kidding, but I knew enough about his domineering nature to realize he was also half serious. He fantasized that the ideal marriage would be to a subservient person who would always put his desires primary and hers secondary.

Most of us have known friendships and marriages where that was the arrangement, and they never work. If one is so strong and aggressive that the other's soul shrivels, unhappiness inevitably results. Some such married couples may stay together for life but that doesn't mean the marriage worked. It simply means that the subservient partner became too weak to function alone and too afraid to get out. Unfortunately, our culture is still backward enough that women who choose to be homemakers are more likely to fall into this trap; but it can work the other way, as illustrated by the amusing novel, *I Don't Know How She Does It* by British critic Allison Pearson. There, Katherine Reddy, a hard-driving manager for an investment-fund, is asked by her hapless husband why she overpays their nanny. "Because I could do without you easier than Paula," she snaps.

Those who want to control everything and deliberately choose someone with weak ego-strength are sure to reap a bitter harvest. The subservient partner or friend becomes increasingly unhappy, less and less fun to be with, less interesting, less lovable, and—most significantly—less able to love.

The best friendships, marriages, business partnerships and parent-child relationships are those that strive for balance. The connections work because each person is getting some needs met, and it is a fairly even swap.

Loving for Selfish Reasons?

For such mutuality to occur, three things must happen. First, the two unashamedly enter the friendship with the hope that some of their desires will be answered, and second, both listen carefully to the data their friend is feeding them about what is desired from the friendship. Finally they both throw themselves into meeting as many of those desires as possible. For thinking Christians, these steps may sound unworkable. The first—going in with specific desires and openly presenting them— is more suspect than the other two. Many of us have been taught rather graphically about the sin of pride, and the concept of telling another in detail what you desire is an unsettling one. It sounds as if we're being encouraged to engage in the thing we should avoid: selfishness.

In many religious circles, a hierarchy of emotions is drawn in which unconditional, or agape love, is at the top, and erotic love at the bottom. Eros (which for most theologians includes sex but is more than sex) is I-love-you-because-I-need-you. According to such writers as C. S. Lewis, it is despicable and disappointing. (For my money, this denigration of Eros is the only place Lewis fails us, which I choose to attribute to the fact that he married late in life. Had he settled into the marriage bed earlier we might have been spared this harshness.)

Another writer, Dwight Small, waxes eloquent on how we are to have unconditional love in marriage:

> Agape is not born of a lover's need, nor does it have its source in the love object. Agape doesn't exist in order to get what it wants but empties itself to give what the other needs. Its motives rise wholly from within its own nature. Agape lives in order to die to self for the blessedness of caring for another, spending for another, spending itself for the sake of the beloved.

That sounds lovely. But it is so idealistic for any human relationship as to be absurd. Only God has such perfect love. That he has loved us in such a way and sent Christ for us is the greatest miracle of the universe. For us to reflect upon it elicits both awe and lifelong gratitude.

But when Christ urges us to love one another, is he saying we are to give ourselves to others year in and year out when we receive nothing in return? Surely not for most of our relationships.

We can pull it off for brief spurts when a friend or mate is ill or in trouble. When we have children we probably come closest to it, but as every parent knows, that's hardly one-way love. You may give more than you get, but a lot of affection comes back from children. And, as every parent also knows, some days it is impossible to give our children anything approaching agape love.

So in human connections we can offer lopsided love for a while, but not forever. Eventually it must get back to something closer to a balance. That is tough to do and deserves some thought.

Let's consider first the difficulty we have in talking about our needs. Why is it so hard to disclose deep yearnings? There are many reasons, but one is that most of us have heard somewhere that if you show yourself to be weak at points, and get emotional about it, people will not like you. But exactly the opposite is true. Assuming that we don't clutch at them, others begin to feel close to us when they know something of our vulnerability.

She Can't Read Your Mind

Here is a man whose marriage is in trouble. As he sits in the therapy group every week telling us what he wants out of life and about the civil war going on in his house, the group members begin to notice that he is telling *us* what he'd like to see happen at home, but he's not telling his wife.

For instance, his best friend dropped dead of a heart attack recently. "I was the last one to stand at the coffin," he tells the group, "the last one to throw dirt in the grave, the last to walk away from the cemetery. That's how important this man was to me. And do you know that my wife didn't even *offer* to go with me to the funeral? I wanted her at my side, and she wasn't there."

The natural question, asked in unison by several members of the group was: "Did you tell her you wanted her to go?"

"Of course not," he barked. "She should have known. After all these years of marriage, do I have to ask for a thing like that?"

We would like our friends and our mates to be so attuned to us that they know our desires instinctively, but that does not happen often; we cannot assume that our partners can read our minds. The tragedy of this man's marriage is that his wife will never be able to meet his needs if she does not know them.

Perhaps, in this case, they have gradually withdrawn from each other out of hurt. At some time he may have asked for her help and been turned down. Hence, he decided not to ask again. And perhaps she offered to be at his side—at some funeral, let us say—and in a bad mood because of some other grievance, he told her to forget it.

You take risks if you become open about your longings. Once in a while the other person will not respond. But it is sad if you stop expressing them because of occasional disappointment and thereby bed down with disappointment as your constant companion.

A Word in Defense of Eros

Let's think for a moment of the specifically sexual part of Eros. Is there something sinful about having sexual longings—which God has evidently put in us? And is it a sin to make love with our mate to fulfill that desire, especially when our mate's desires are also being met? Because God not only gave us the longing but also made sex to be intensely pleasurable, he presumably expected us to enjoy it. Let's be honest, then: there is a large element of self-gratification in erotic love.

Here is a plant foreman who works the 4–11 shift and comes home late at night. He is tired and stressed, and at such times he gets a little obsessive about sex. So he is already thinking about making love as he drives into the garage. He knows that his wife will be in bed reading and waiting for him, probably naked under the covers. When he crawls under and feels her curves, he is immediately aroused. He watches the rhythm of her arousal and adapts his actions to it. But he craves her body. It is that simple.

Is such raw animal passion wrong? Some theologians and other thinkers believe so, calling Eros, "I-love-you-because-I-need-you." He is, in one psychologist's words, "seeking self-gratification by means of another," and with such a definition the writer supposes he is pointing out how evil pure erotic desire is. But it is not evil when rightly used: it is wonderful. It is I-love-you-*and*-I-need-you.

With the exception of a few radical feminists, most women do not see such desire as evil. In fact I cannot recall a woman ever telling me that she was sorry to have a man aroused by her looks. Sometimes women say that an attractive body can create problems occasionally, and naturally they are offended if men harass them, treat them as mere sexual objects, or try to push themselves on them. They often say that their husbands should take more time. But raw animal passion? More women complain to me about its *absence* in their husbands than about its presence.

Let us agree, then, that pleasure by means of the one we love is not inherently bad. It is only when we take our pleasure at the *expense* of others that Eros becomes manipulation.

Well-meaning Christians such as Gary Small who go on and on about agape love take a wrong turn (and a rather serious one) by ignoring the crucial signpost of Christ's second great commandment. There our Lord does not urge us to love our neighbor *instead* of ourselves—denigrating ourselves by giving and giving when we receive nothing. Rather, we are to love the other *as* ourselves. Such a statement assumes a very high self-regard.

More about that in the next chapter.

CHAPTER 19

Self-Worth: A Requirement for Intimacy

*Friendship is seldom lasting but between equals. . . .
Benefits which cannot be repaid and obligations
which cannot be discharged are not commonly found
to increase affection. They excite gratitude indeed
and heighten veneration, but commonly take away
that easy freedom and familiarity of intercourse
without which . . . there cannot be friendship.*

—Samuel Johnson

THE BRILLIANCE OF JESUS'S COMMANDMENT TO LOVE
your neighbor as yourself is that it states so com-
pactly a profound psychological fact: that identity
and intimacy go together, and to be happy we must
have both. We can't have a very positive self-perception if we're not loving and being loved. And we
can't be good at love unless we have healthy self-
worth. The two develop in tandem. Occasionally a

client will say to people like me, "I don't date or
have friends, and I'm not ready to do so—I first
want to concentrate in therapy on understanding
myself, then I'll try finding some friends." But we
can't understand ourselves in a vacuum, without
some reactions of other people. Nor can we love
well if we are loaded down with guilt and self-
loathing.

In working with such persons, I set out to con-
vince them that God created them. And if that is
true, they can't be so terrible. The next step is to tell
them that God loves them. God loved them
enough to send his Son to die for them. *That* is
agape love. Furthermore, God knows them by
name, and nothing they could do could make God
love them more than he does right now. If they can
respond to that, and establish a personal relationship with Christ, it can improve their view of
themselves immeasurably.

Either a Damaging or a Creative Circle

One of the self-perpetuating circles that we therapists like to see in our clients is this: The better
your self-image, the better friends you are likely to
choose; then, in turn, as you have better relationships, your self-esteem will rise. It is building success on success each time you round the circle.

But the corollary is that the worse you think of
yourself, the more likely you are to choose jerks for
friends; thus your interpersonal relations will go
poorly, with the result that your self-perception
will deteriorate even more.

How does a psychotherapist try to break that
cycle? Two ways, basically. The first is to try to

establish in the counseling room a good relationship. Perhaps it is the best relationship the client has. Perhaps it is the *only* one.

But that is not enough, because people who depend on the approval of others for their confidence will be disappointed, and what's more, their craving for approval can ruin a friendship by overloading it.

M. Esther Harding is a good analyst of this rubber crutch:

> When someone is uncertain of himself, always needing approval and support of others and being unduly depressed by their criticism, it means that he has no valid criterion of value from within himself. If he is disapproved of, he feels crushed; if he is not noticed, he ceases to exist; and if he is praised, he is in the seventh heaven of elation. He has little sense of his personal value, though he may give the appearance of being exceedingly egotistic; since he is always "fishing" for praise. He purrs and preens himself when it is given, literally basking in an atmosphere of approval, while he usually goes away by himself to hide his hurt if the desired notice is not forthcoming. His center of gravity is not in himself, but outside in other people.

So the lesson is clear: a good relationship will help build self-image, but you cannot depend on others for nearly all your sense of worth. It must come from within you.

Accepting the Unacceptable Within Ourselves

I once wrote a book on the subject of self-perception, titled *Confidence*. There I tried to say that the better we can know ourselves the better we're going to feel about who we are—the more at peace we'll be. Not everyone would agree with that. Some, for instance, hesitate to enter therapy because they're afraid they'll discover frightening and degenerate pockets deep inside and end up worse off than before.

But the only time therapy hurts more than it helps is when people bolt midway through. In such cases, they sometimes are indeed worse off, because we've uncovered negative material without exorcising its power. But I've never had clients who stuck with it until the work was complete who went away thinking less of themselves rather than more. To name a thing is to take away much of its power. Self-acceptance doesn't mean that we'll like all that we find within, or that we'll stop working to improve our faults. There is a difference between encouraging the sinful tendencies within us and accepting the fact that they are there.

Freud's Septic Tank

Sigmund Freud realized, brilliantly, that in psychotherapy it is necessary to delve down into the world of our forgotten memories and repressed desires, which he called the unconscious. Freud's theories have been dismissed by many in the new schools of thought about human consciousness: the neuropsychiatrists and evolutionary psychologists. They think that the unconscious is nonexistent. But I find that many of Freud's descriptions of the inner world match up both with what I discover in myself and what I see in my clients.

The difficulty in Freud's system is that it is too bleak. An atheist and a pessimist, he looked at the unconscious as a rather frightening place. He thought therapy's work was like taking the lid off a septic tank, where there were all manner of perverted sexual desires and unconscionable aggression. Someone has said that Freud went down deeper, stayed down longer, and came up dirtier than any psychologist since.

On the other hand, Carl Jung, the son of a pastor, believed that when people who have led repressed lives begin exploring the unconscious they may indeed find a layer of sludge at the top. But when they get past that, the unconscious is a beautiful, rich world, from which come color, music, myth, and creativity. I much prefer this view over Freud's. Jung even felt that it is in the unconscious that we experience God most fully. For that reason Jung spent a great deal of time listening to his patients' accounts of their dreams. Why? In order to aid them in knowing the hidden richness within. He also paid attention to his own dreams for the same reason, and occasionally he even looked to them to help him make decisions.

I have found that many of my clients arrive at our offices with no idea of who they are. All they know is that they don't like themselves much, that they're in a lot of emotional pain, and that their relationships have a way of turning to ashes. Such people with little confidence sometimes require a safe place where they can begin to talk about their buried experiences and shameful memories, along with the conviction that they are strange and unlovable. Eventually, as they stare down the skeletons in the closet and as the skeletons begin to lose their power over them, people often find they can gain courage. And because I'm not shocked by what they are telling me they find it doesn't sound so shocking to themselves. Hopefully they will eventually gain the ability to confide in another person the way they are confiding in me.

Understanding Your Wants and Desires

Not only is it important to understand your dark side, it is also essential to get a grasp of your hopes, your desires, your particular pleasures, what you like, and how you're different from others in these needs. Here again, I often find that new clients have little knowledge of what they want from life—what might bring them joy. I will sometimes send them home with a sheet of paper that has the heading "20 Things I Like to Do," with twenty blank lines. Their homework is to write down twenty at one sitting. I tell them the items can be small, like soaking in a hot tub or watching some television program.

The first few times I tried this, I was stunned that clients would usually come back the following week with only five or six items on the list. That showed how out of contact they were with their spontaneous selves. Small wonder that they were unhappy. They had no idea what *would* make them happy. And, small wonder that they were unhappy in their relationships, because how could they reveal their needs and desires to their close friends and mates if they didn't know what they wanted?

One of the tasks of good self-understanding is to analyze the ways you are unique. That makes it possible to negotiate with friends and mates much better because you can put on the table some preferences and aversions.

So, selfish as it may seem, the best friendships occur when two people know their idiosyncrasies well and are able to explain to their friends or mates their preferences. That doesn't mean, of course, that anyone is going to get everything they want in a friendship, but it helps to start with a clear understanding of yourself.

Adjusting the Balance

If there is to be a balance of self-regard and regard for your friend, the relationship will probably require some tinkering over the years. Joan and Meredith have been friends since college. They live two hundred miles apart and see each other only two or three times a year, so most of their communication is by telephone or e-mail. For several months Meredith and her husband have been at odds. With two small children, both still in diapers, she doesn't have much diversion. So she bombards Joan with e-mails—more than Joan has time to answer. And Meredith frequently calls Joan at work; mostly to complain, it seems to Joan. She has lots of sympathy and has been willing to spend most of their communications hearing about Meredith and offering as much encouragement as she can. After several months of this, however, she is beginning to dread hearing from this friend who in the past has been dear. When Joan tries to tell Meredith a little about her life—its highs and lows—Meredith makes almost no response and often interrupts by getting self-referential again.

Should Joan stop returning her friend's calls and answering her e-mails? Certainly not. At least not without attempting to adjust the mix. When a connection has been happy for so many years, you don't immediately throw it overboard.

What is necessary is that they have some conversation about this. The time and place should be right. Hopefully it will be a time when neither is in crisis. And it will go much better if it is face-to-face. So some weekend it will be worth Joan's driving the two hundred miles.

During the weekend she might say something like this. "Know what, Meredith? One reason I came up was to talk about our friendship. We've been tight so long, and you're terribly important to me. But lately it hasn't been as good for me, partly because it hasn't seemed as if you were tuned in much to what's going on at my end. I realize this year has been hellish, and I've been glad to have the conversation pretty much one-way for a while. Lord knows I feel for you and want to be all the support I can be from a distance.

"I'm sure my life looks a lot better than yours, and it probably is at the moment. But I have difficulties, too. I would like to talk to you about them and get some advice and help from you at times. When I try to talk about what's going on it seems as if you interrupt with more stuff about yourself. I thought you might not even be aware of this—or that I'm not seeing it right. I don't know. I've had to screw up my courage to say this, but I really love you, Meredith. What do you think?"

If the expression and re-expression of your wishes was the only part of these transactions, you would indeed be selfish and unchristian, and the friendship would be barren. But there is another step.

Love, Honor, and Negotiate

Toni is happily married to a crane operator. She and Douglas have been together for many years, and one would think that any romantic gloss would have worn off by now. But they still hold hands as they walk through the mall and anytime they are together—though they may be talking to other people at a party—they appear to be tuned in to one another and will smile at each other across the room.

This is all the more remarkable because anyone doing premarital testing on this couple would have rated them as not very compatible. She loves classical music; he prefers jazz. She's a college graduate; he dropped out after two years. She is five years older than he.

"So how do you account for all this happiness?" I asked her.

"We're very honest with each other."

"You mean you have no secrets?"

"No, that's not what I mean, though there are probably almost none. What I'm talking about is that we're up front with each other about what we like and don't like, what we need from one another, how we could adjust our friendship so we're meeting each other's wants and desires better."

"Don't those desires sometimes clash?"

"Of *course*." She laughed. "They clash all the time, and that's when we bargain. I read a marriage book once that had a chapter titled, 'Love, Honor, and Negotiate.'"

She went on to talk mostly about Douglas. (She never referred to him as "Doug," always "Douglas.")

"Douglas may not be the most handsome man in the world, and he'll never be president of his company, but if he ever died, I'd be devastated. I could take care of myself fine—I don't mean that. I mean that Douglas seems to have made a study of me, and he knows how to make me happy.

"Music, for instance, is a big part of my life and although he doesn't love symphonies the way I do, he doesn't seem to mind going at all. And when he brings home a new CD he knows I'd like, he's happy—I guess because he sees how happy he's making me.

"Or take sex. Some of my friends complain that their husbands are clumsy lovers. Not Douglas. He knows my body like a musician knows the violin, and he plays me for all I'm worth. He takes his time, he romances me, he laughs and teases with me. We play in bed. I can't imagine being more fulfilled sexually."

Is Toni's happiness due to being married to such a great guy? Not necessarily. Many other women are married to what seem to be good men and are frustrated in their marriages. Why then is Toni so compatible with her husband? For several reasons. One, she has found a man who is evidently very much at ease living in his own skin—he has confidence. Two, both have unashamedly entered this marriage in order to have some of their needs met. Toni has good self-understanding and articulates her preferences well. Douglas, in turn, evidently understands his emotional makeup and clearly communicates his desires to her. Three, both listen carefully to the data their mate is feeding them about what they like. Four, they compromise. And finally, they throw themselves into meeting as many of the beloved's needs as possible. It is a mutual exchange.

CHAPTER 20

The Art
of Adaptation

Love is seldom spontaneous, instant, dynamic. It usually takes considerable time to create. It results from work, from thinking, from promoting equality, from being able to cope and adapt.
—William Lederer

In order to correct an overemphasis on denying oneself in some religious circles, I have spent time in the previous two chapters defending the virtue of learning as much about yourself as possible so it can be clear, both to you and to your friend, what you'd like from the connection.

Having said that, I now wish to turn the coin over and observe that many friendships and marriages fail because of selfishness. And just as it is important to ascertain your desires, it is crucial to bend to the desires of your friend.

It is a curious phenomenon how we begin a courtship, for instance, with such intense focus on the beloved and such intense effort to learn all the other's fears and dreams and every little preference and taste. Our eyes and ears are open, we watch carefully, and we log everything in the memory bank. Then with all that in mind, we resolve to do the things that will make our beloved happy, no matter how inconvenient. We get lots of pleasure from it. But years pass and something terrible happens. Our keen watchfulness turns to indifference.

In marriage seminars I frequently quote Art Sueltz's chronicle of the stages of the common cold in seven years of marriage:

> First year: "Sugar, I'm worried about my little baby girl. You've got a bad sniffle. I want to put you in the hospital for a complete checkup. I know the food is lousy, but I've arranged for your meals to be sent in from Rossini's."
>
> Second year: "Listen, honey, I don't like the sound of that cough. I've called Dr. Miller and he's going to rush right over. Now will you go to bed like a good girl just for me, please?"
>
> Third year: "Maybe you'd better lie down, honey. Nothing like a little rest if you're feeling bad. I'll bring you something to eat. Have we got any soup in the house?"
>
> Fourth year: "Look, dear. Be sensible. After you've fed the kids and washed the dishes, you'd better go to bed early."
>
> Fifth year: "Why don't you take a couple of aspirin?"

Sixth year: "If you'd just gargle or something instead of sitting around barking like a seal."

Seventh year: "Can't you stop your sneezing? What are you trying to do, give me pneumonia?"

The willingness to sacrifice for the sake of the one you love—to sublimate your preferences at times—is imperative for a long-term friendship. One woman who has had a splendid, long marriage said, "Ours is a 25/75 marriage. Sometimes the 75 comes from me and sometimes it comes from my husband. But we don't keep track." And a physician who has had a smooth thirty-four-year partnership with another doctor said wryly, "For an equal partnership to work, you've got to do 60 percent of the work, because your partner will discount at least 10 percent of it."

Self-Transcendence

To find the fullest meaning in life, we must be at peace with ourselves, but we must also get outside ourselves. The psychiatrist Viktor Frankl frequently asked his patients who were struggling with their sufferings, "For whose sake do you do so?" He asked the question because it is only when we begin to live for someone beyond ourselves, Frankl contended, that we find happiness.

Jesus nowhere urged self-contempt, but neither does he advocate self-worship, as do certain pop psychologists. How do we avoid pride? Two ways. First, we keep before us a clear vision of the Holy: "You shall love the Lord your God with all your heart, and with all your soul, and with all your mind." And second, we get outside our own skin by loving another: "You shall love your neighbor as yourself" (Matt. 22:36-38).

As in most things, moderation and balance is the key, and we keep a balance by attending to the needs of our friends at least as much as to our own.

Toni, whose marriage to Douglas I described earlier, was on to something important when she said that people who are going to stay close should "love, honor, and negotiate."

Joshua and Harry, who play racquetball twice a week, have this regular dispute: Joshua likes to play singles, Harry prefers doubles. Joshua prefers singles in part so the two of them can have a talk over coffee when the game is over. Harry likes to play doubles because he thinks it's more fun to kid around with not one but three other guys.

They argue about this every week, and it is becoming a sore point, causing some serious ill-feeling. The reason is this: they don't know each other's motivations. All they know is that they are having these disputes. It is remarkable how often the reasons for such preferences are withheld but are the underlying burr under the saddle. What will help the situation? They can clearly state their preferences, such as "I like Stewart and Jarrett, but it means a lot to be alone with you for a while. I can be more honest with you over coffee than with three other guys." Harry may be touched by that and say, "Really? I had no idea that's why you preferred singles. Those talks mean a lot to me, too. Now that I think about it, let's do it that way."

If both have strong reasons to stick to their guns, then they try something else. Negotiation. Compromise.

In many marriages, one of the partners likes socializing more than the other. I happen to be something of a hermit whose idea of a fine evening is reading a book in bed, whereas Diane loves going to parties. The result is that we probably socialize more than I would choose on my own, and less than she would choose. We compromise cheerfully because we love each other like crazy and as much as possible we want to fulfill our partner's desires.

PART VII

CONCLUSION

CHAPTER 21

You Can Be Lovable

Love never ends.
   —1 Corinthians 13:8

HENRY DRUMMOND ONCE WROTE A CELEBRATED essay on love that he titled "The Greatest Thing in the World." I have never met anyone who disagreed with the axiom that love is the finest experience in the world, but I frequently talk to people who despair of ever finding it. They are convinced that they are unlovable, and indeed their track records seem to bear out those beliefs.

But in years of counseling I have never met a person who was permanently disabled for warm nurturing connections with others. It is possible you have developed some rough edges that complicate your relationships and get you into trouble. Perhaps you must learn some new habits, but at the core you are fully capable of becoming lovable.

On Saturdays, it is frequently my habit to enjoy a long lunch with some former client. I usually return to the office glad to be a counselor, for these people, many of whom were in desperate crises when they began therapy, I find to be happier and better equipped to deal with their worlds.

It is often humbling to talk with these old friends, because they have made so much progress without me! Sometimes I had discharged them with misgivings, but now they are functioning well and are miles down the road. Why? Without exception it is because they have connected with one or two persons who have loved them and whom they have loved back. They have discovered the friendship factor.

Here is a young systems analyst who has been shy and withdrawn all his life. He came to us because his depression was overpowering and he feared that something was about to crack.

It was three years ago that he had his last session, and at that time I knew there was some danger that he might relapse and require more therapy. But here he is sitting across the table telling me about the ski club of which he is treasurer. Where on earth did he find the courage to take on a job like that, I ask.

"I guess I've changed a lot," he replies. "Not that I'm the party type—never will be that. But I'm not afraid of people anymore, and that's probably because of a couple of friendships I've developed at the office. I began looking for other shy people I might get to know, and one older fellow and I really hit it off. He's also a skier, and we do a lot of things together, but the best thing is having some-body to talk to. I mean *really* talk to. I can tell him anything without getting a lecture from him, and he confides in me a lot, too.

"You'll be interested to know that I've got a girl-friend now, too. We haven't dated very long, and sometimes I'm scared to death, but it's my friend-ship with Harv that's given me the courage to relate to women."

It works every time.

Anyone who dares to try the principles of love, and who will apply them to new friendships, begins to experience self-assuring power. That new confidence enables them to try other bonding.

It has been the assumption of this book that you can have a life filled with love. No matter how lacking in the social graces, no matter how poorly suited you feel your personality is for friendship, you can be lovable. And unless you live in an iso-lated cabin in the Yukon, you can establish lasting connections with other people.

Love comes not to those who are merely good-looking or talented. True, beauty and talent will attract new people initially, but it never creates love. Love is something you *do,* and if you will employ the basic laws outlined in this book, you can have great friendships.

Love's Power
In 1925 a tiny sanitarium for mental patients was established on a farm outside Topeka, Kansas. At a time when the "rest cure" was in vogue in psychia-try, a team of physicians—a father and his two sons recently out of medical school—determined to

create a family atmosphere among their patients. The nurses were given specific directions on how they were to behave toward specific patients: "Let them know that you value and like them." "Be kind but firm with this woman—don't let her become worse."

Those young doctors were Karl and Will Menninger, and the Menninger Clinic, using such "revolutionary" methods, has become world famous. More psychiatrists journey to Topeka for special training than to any other such institution in the world.

Karl Menninger (who also taught an adult class at his church most of his life), summing up, said: "Love is the medicine for the sickness of mankind. We can live if we have love."

The same message comes from another psychiatrist to whom I referred earlier, who discovered it in another setting. During World War II, Viktor Frankl was interned by the Germans for more than three years. He was moved from one concentration camp to another. He even survived several months at Auschwitz. Dr. Frankl said he learned early that one way to survive was to shave every day, no matter how sick you were, even if you had to use a piece of broken glass as a razor. For every morning, as the prisoners stood for review, the sickly ones who would not be able to work that day were sent to the gas chambers. If you were shaven, and your face looked ruddier for it, your chances of escaping death—at least for that day—were better.

Their bodies wasted away on the daily fare of 10½ ounces of bread and 1½ pints of thin gruel. They slept on bare board tiers seven feet wide,

nine men to a tier. The nine men shared two blan-
kets. Three shrill whistles awoke them for work at
3:00 A.M.

One morning as they marched out to lay rail-
road ties in the frozen ground miles from the
camp, the accompanying guards kept shouting and
driving them with the butts of their rifles. Anyone
with sore feet supported himself on his neighbor's
arm. The man next to Frankl, hiding his mouth
behind his upturned collar, whispered:

"If our wives could see us now! I do hope they
are better off in their camps and don't know what
is happening to us."

Frankl writes:

> That brought thoughts of my own wife to
> mind. And as we stumbled on for miles, slip-
> ping on icy spots, supporting each other time
> and again, dragging one another up and
> onward, nothing was said, but we both knew;
> each of us was thinking of his wife.
> Occasionally I looked at the sky, where the stars
> were fading and the pink light of the morning
> was beginning to spread behind a dark bank of
> clouds. But my mind clung to [that picture of
> my wife] . . . imagining it with an uncanny
> acuteness. I heard her answering me, saw her
> smile, her frank and encouraging look.
>
> A thought transfixed me: for the first time
> in my life I saw the truth as it is set into song
> by so many poets, proclaimed as the final
> wisdom by so many thinkers. The truth—
> that love is the ultimate and the highest goal
> to which [we] . . . can aspire. Then I grasped

the meaning of the greatest secret that human poetry and human thought and belief have to impart: . . . salvation . . . is through love and in love.

It is perhaps the most powerful thought anyone can have. When we remember the primacy of love, and believe in our almost unlimited capacities for giving and receiving it, life can take on a vast joyfulness. Teilhard de Chardin once wrote: "Someday, after we have mastered the winds and the waves, the tides, and gravity, we will harness for God the energies of love, and then for the second time in the history of the world . . . [we] will have discovered fire."

THE FRIENDSHIP FACTOR
How to Get Closer to the People You Care For

Large-quantity purchases or custom editions of this book are available at a discount from the publisher. For more information, contact the sales department at Augsburg Fortress, Publishers, 1-800-328-4648, or write to: Sales Director, Augsburg Fortress, Publishers, P.O. Box 1209, Minneapolis, MN 55440-1209.

Scripture passages are from the New Revised Standard Version of the Bible, copyright © 1946, 1952, 1971, 1989 by the Division of Christian Education of the National Council of the Churches of Christ in the USA. Used by permission.

Scripture passages are from the Good News Bible—Old Testament: copyright © 1976 American Bible Society; New Testament: copyright © 1966, 1971, 1976 by the American Bible Society. Used by permission.

Scripture passages are from the New American Standard Bible, copyright © 1960, 1962, 1963, 1968, 1971, 1972, 1973, 1975, 1977 The Lockman Foundation. Used by permission.

Scripture passages are from the New American Bible, copyright © 1970 by the Confraternity of Christian Doctrine, Washington, DC, and are used by permission of the copyright owner. All rights reserved.

ISBN 0-8066-3571-1

Cover and book design by Michelle L. N. Cook, cover art from Artville.

The paper used in this publication meets the minimum requirements of American National Standard for Information Sciences—Permanence of Paper for Printed Library Materials, ANSI Z329.48-1984. ∞ ™

Manufactured in the U.S.A.

08   07   06   4   5   6   7   8   9   10